ARCHBISHOP LUIS AUGUSTO CASTRO

ECOLOGY OF THE FOREST
ECOLOGY OF THE SOUL

GREEN AMAZONIA
BREATH OF THE SPIRIT

Translated from Spanish
by Cecilia Castro Lee Ph.D
And Carey Phillip Lee Ed.S.

Luis Augusto Castro, Bogotá, 1942
Archbishop of Tunja, Colombia, South America
Former Bishop of the Apostolic Vicariate of
San Vicente del Caguán-Puerto Leguízamo
Colombia, South America

Spanish First Edition 1995:   *Ecología del bosque Ecología del alma*
Spanish Second Edition 2015: *Ecología del bosque Ecología del alma*
English Translation 2016:   *Ecology of the Forest Ecology of the Soul*

ISBN:978-958-8463-38-4
Photography
Cover page: Dr. Miguel Ángel Piñeros
Illustrations: *Colombia Amazónica -Diccionario dos peixes do Brasil-*
Gran Enciclopedia Didáctica Ilustrada,
V. 6 and 7- *El Gran Libro de Colombia,* V.1 and 2.

Printed in Colombia
Editorial Kimpres S.A.S
Phone: 413 68 84
January 2016
Bogotá, Colombia
South America

CONTENTS

TRANSLATORS' NOTE

Luis Augusto Castro is presently the Archbishop of Tunja, Colombia, and he also serves as the President of the Bishops Conference of Colombia. He has a Ph.D. in Missionary Theology from the Pontifical Javeriana University in Bogotá. He is the author of sixty books written in Spanish, several of which have been translated into Italian and Portuguese. This is his first work to be translated into English. *Ecology of the Forest, Ecology of the Soul* was inspired by his twelve years of work as a Missionary Bishop in the States of Caquetá and Putumayo in the Amazon Region of Colombia where he was immersed in the culture and experienced life's daily challenges.

Archbishop Castro takes the reader through the biological diversity, flora, fauna, natural phenomena, and the socio-political trials of Amazonia in Colombia. At the same time, the reader partakes in a spiritual growth journey. This book addresses faith and spirituality through the beauty of nature, the miracle of life, the struggle for survival, and the ecological concerns of the Amazon rain forest.

In the original Spanish edition, published in 1995, the author emphasized the importance of preserving the Rain Forest while nourishing the human spirit. We are proud to share his stories and concerns with the English speaking audience. As we translated this book into English, we endeavored to keep the author's voice alive with fidelity to his text and the author's intentions.

Simple in style and rich in content, this book is a literary piece filled with wisdom and sprinkled with humor and grace.

The English citations from Pope Francis's *Laudato si* Encyclical (2015) are taking directly from Vatican documents.

We thank the Misereor organization for a grant which made the publication of this English translation possible. We gratefully acknowledge Dr. Marjorie Snipes for her reading of the translation and her words of encouragement. A debt of gratitude is owed to Dr. Eleanor Hoomes for her reading and valuable suggestions. We wish to thank our children and families for their never-failing encouragement and support.

Cecilia Castro Lee
Carey Phillip Lee
Carrollton, Georgia, January 6, 2016

INTRODUCTION

I n the year 1541 when Francisco de Orellana began his journey through the fabulous Amazon River, he had no idea of the incredible world that he was about to discover.

The journey that you are about to begin as you read this book has little of Orellana's amazing exploits. In the simplicity of this book's style of writing, however, you may be impressed by some of the things that awed Orellana on his expedition from Quito to the mouth of the Amazon River in 1542.

Forty-two years earlier, Vicente Yañez Pinzón had reached the mouth of the river and had named it *Santa María de la Mar Dulce,* Saint Mary of the Sea of Fresh Water. Thus, he left a mark of faith in God and a love of the Virgin Mary on this unique place.

But then again, all of Amazonia is a manifestation of faith. Throughout this rain forest you will discover the imprint of The Living God.

Hence as you travel through this book, you will not merely advance horizontally through a jungle filled with creatures, but you will also advance vertically as you listen to and praise their Creator. This is what the title of this book, *Ecology of the Forest, Ecology of the Soul*, wishes to bring to mind.

This book gathers my observations when I was Bishop of the Apostolic Vicariate of San Vicente-Puerto Leguízamo in the Amazon Region of Colombia between1986 and1998.

I dedicate this Second Edition to Pope Francis. He has given us ecological teachings that are both delightful and urgent in his Encyclical, *Laudato Si.* (LS, May 24, 2015)

Have a good journey!

Luis Augusto Castro
Archbishop of Tunja
Colombia, South America

> *"St. Francis of Assisi helps us to see that an integral ecology calls for openness to categories which transcend the language of mathematics and biology, and take us to the heart of what it is to be human. Just as happens when we fall in love with someone, whenever St. Francis would gaze at the sun, the moon or the smallest of animals, he burst into song, drawing all other creatures into his praise. He communed with all creation, even preaching to the flowers, inviting them ' to praise the Lord, just as if they were endowed with reason.' "(LS 11)*

THE
STRANGLING
EPIPHYTES

As it happens, even in the best of families, the differences among members can be enormous. This is what occurs in the family called epiphytes, plants that sprout and grow on the trunks of trees.

There are beautiful epiphytes, such as orchids, which inspired one of the First Ladies of Colombia to organize an expedition to collect a great number of orchids from the jungle.

There are also some terrifying ones, such as the strangling epiphytes. After settling to live and flourish on the tree where they have germinated, they begin to grow powerful roots that little by little surround the tree in a malignant grip until they strangle it.

In the end, as expected, the strangled tree disappears and leaves in its place a dark hole bordered by the root formation of the ungrateful strangling epiphytes.

Watch out for the strangling epiphytes that may grow in your life. Some make advances as innocent orchids and end up draining your spirit and withering your life.

St. Augustine was a special Saint since he had to divest himself of a good number of strangling epiphytes when he decided to give more attention to his inner life. It was not a question of vanity. It was a matter of faith. From deep inside, he came in contact with his true self and the truth of God.

No wonder he wrote: "The exterior Master became interior in order to call us from the exterior to the interior."

SMALL THINGS ENHANCE LIFE

A few years back it was quite fashionable to praise small things by saying: "Small things are lovely."

I'm not interested in knowing if small things are lovely or not, but small things in the world of the jungle are vital.

I will call upon the mushrooms, the lichens, and the insects as my witnesses.

All of the enormous trees of Amazonia, the solemn palm trees and other inhabitants, would suffer bitter times if these co-workers which I have summoned weren't hidden somewhere.

It is a fact that all of the debris that falls from the trees would be useless rubble and a hindrance if these minuscule organisms weren't around to accomplish a vital task.

They are charged with transforming dead organic waste into consumable nutrients which will serve to bring forth renewed life.

Thanks to them, the cycle repeats itself and the continuity of life, even that of the gigantic beings, remains ensured.

In order to give life, we rely on the minute. This is also the style of God.

Jesus beautifully manifested this when addressing his Father in a familiar tone, He said to Him: "Father, Lord of heaven and earth! I thank you because you have shown the unlearned what you have hidden from the wise." (Luke 10, 21)

> "It may well disturb us to learn of the extinction of mammals or birds, since they are more visible. But the efficient functioning of ecosystems also requires fungi, algae, worms, insects, reptiles and an innumerable variety of microorganisms. Some less numerous species, although generally unseen, play a critical role in maintaining the equilibrium of a particular place." (LS 34)

CLIMB THE
TREE OF LIFE

I ts name is *Bactris* and it's a palm tree. It is thorny, apparently because it does not like for those gathering species from the terrestrial habitat to climb its trunk.

The unfortunate thing is that on the top, there is a fruit that is quite delicious.

The Yanomami Indians, however, know how to get around the obstacle of these piercing thorns.

They plant a fast-growing tree right next to the palm tree. When it reaches sufficient height, they climb up beyond the thorny part and cross over to the palm tree in order to collect the appetizing fruit.

You should learn from the Yanomami Indians.

The fruit of salvation has been obstructed by the thorns of sin. But, just beside the thorny tree, another redeeming tree has grown: the tree of the cross. Climb it.

Now that I recall, St. Rosa of Lima suggested something similar when she said: "Other than the cross there is no other stairway to go up to heaven."

> "Human beings too are creatures of this world, enjoying a right to life and happiness, endowed with unique dignity. So we cannot fail to consider the effects on people's lives of environmental deterioration, current models of development and the throwaway culture." (LS 43)

REPAIRABLE WOUNDS AND FATAL WOUNDS

The indigenous people know how to live with the jungle without inflicting fatal wounds upon it. In fact, the damage that they cause soon heals and the jungle grows back more fertile.

The wounds from the natives are repairable because the extension of the jungle that is burned or destroyed isn't so large as to prevent insects and birds from flying from one side to the other.

The flight of birds and insects guarantees that seeds and pollen can be taken back and forth in order to restore the spaces that have been left empty.

The limited wounds made by the indigenous people allow for the creation of a living bridge between opposite borders of the affected terrain.

Almost all of the wounds which human beings inflict upon one another are similar to those caused by the natives to the forest. They are repairable wounds, although at first glance they may appear to be mortal.

I want to invite you to become a living bridge between opposing sides of an affected human terrain.

"But, how is this possible?" You may wonder, "Am I by chance a bird?" In a certain way you are. St. Augustine explains this in a beautiful way: "Our love is the wings."

By loving we fly to God and by loving we fly to the opposing sides of wounded people, motivating reconciliation.

"Each year sees the disappearance of thousands of plant and animal species which we will never know, which our children will never see, because they have been lost forever. The great majority become extinct for reasons related to human activity." (LS 33)

FRAGILITY IN SEARCH OF PROTECTION

W ho would believe it, after seeing such corpulent trees and such thick vegetation?

But, it is an absolute truth that the Amazon soil is fragile and extremely thin.

That is why the soil asks, pleads, and implores that no one cut the shelter that protects it, which is the vegetal covering called a canopy. When the trees are cut and the canopy is missing erosion takes place at an incredible speed.

When water, which in itself is good, falls on unprotected ground, it sweeps away sediments leaving the soil impoverished.

Moreover, the resulting fluvial sediments bring about immense river floods. These overloading deposits elevate the river bed, form sand banks, and may alter the course of navigation channels.

A few years ago a book entitled, *The Sacred Canopy*, was released.

From it we can see that, in addition to the natural canopy that protects the Amazon soil, there is another canopy. It is The Sacred Canopy which protects those who are fragile and weak.

Feeling helpless, St, Augustine appealed to this Sacred Canopy. Let us unite in his plea: "Lord, have pity of me, a featherless chick, so that, fallen on the road as I am, may I not be trampled by passersby."

If you think that this is also your case, you may add: "Do not forget, Lord, he who had forgotten you."

> *"Certain places need greater protection because of their immense importance for the global ecosystem, or because they represent important water reserves and thus safeguard other forms of life. Let us mention, for example, those richly biodiverse lungs of our planet which are the Amazon and the Congo basins, or the great aquifers and glaciers. We know how important these are for the entire earth and for the future of humanity." (LS 37-38)*

THE RIVER THAT FLOWS DOWN THE MOUNTAIN

The rivers of Amazonia are varied. They are often classified as white, black, or clear. Those carrying the greatest richness are the ones that descend from the Andean mountains.

More than white, these rivers are perceived as being yellow. This isn't due to dirt or pollution. It's because the rivers bring down fertile materials and organic life from the mountains which become wonderful nutrients for all of the fish.

These sediments in suspension which give the river its muddy appearance, far from being a sign of contamination, are a sign of life for the species that inhabit the waters.

They are indeed precious and fortifying gifts that flow down from the mountain.

Moses went up the mountain, where he met God face to face, and when he came down his face looked radiant. He also descended the mountain with a divine and fortifying message.

This river that flows down from the mountain is symbolic of a man who reaches out to his brothers and sisters after having encountered The Lord on the heights of The Mountain. In other words, he has lived a formidable experience with God.

Thus this enlightened person can proclaim in unison with John the Apostle:

Which we have heard,
Which we have seen with our own eyes,
Which we looked upon and our hands have touched
Concerning the Word of life,
What we have seen and heard
We proclaim also to you. (John 1, 3)

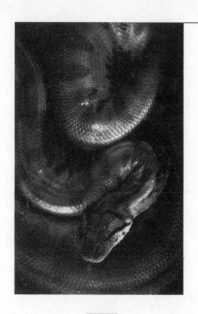

LOATHING
LIGHT

The *Verrugosa* or Bushmaster (*Lachesis muta or the Silent Fate*) is a highly poisonous serpent that can reach up to four meters (thirteen feet) in length. Bushmasters live hidden in the depths of the jungle amid shadows that are so dense that everything is dark.

The Bushmaster is a very aggressive snake. When it gets furious it rushes after its victim. This fact is not deemed extraordinary as far as life in the jungle is concerned. But the curious thing is that the Bushmaster loathes light itself.

Actually, there is a popular belief that this viper furiously chases any beam of light. Therefore, it is dangerous to walk with a lantern at night in the middle of the jungle.

Do not let the Bushmaster or any type of serpent frighten you. Instead, accept the challenge that Christ presents to you: "May your light shine before people, so that they will see the good things that you do which praise your Father who is in heaven." (Matthew 5, 16)

AN
INEXPENSIVE
SUTURE

We are not talking about a rural hospital in the middle of the jungle. The Indigenous people fashion their cost-effective medical suture in a very original way.

Who has never seen an endless line of ants on the way to an anthill with each one carrying its own little leaf cut from a tree by its powerful pinchers?

Thus far, everything is normal. We should add that these ants are workers and soldiers at the same time.

Now we will get to the matter of the suture. When a native gets a cut, he grabs an ant and places it to join the two sides of the wound. Then, the little insect closes its pinchers, and the wound is sutured.

Obviously the ant is not going to remain there with its pinchers closed until the wound heals.

So the injured native pulls the ant's head off of the body leaving the pinchers holding the wound as an effective and inexpensive clasp.

This ant has the wonderful power to bring forth the image of Jesus to our mind and heart.

He cured the open wound caused by sin. He also accepted death in order to heal the wounded. And, He served as a suture to unite His people.

As the Apostle Paul explains in a magnificent way: "But now, in union with Christ Jesus, you who used to be far away have been brought near by the sacrificial death of Christ." (Ephesians 2, 13)

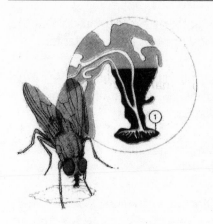

TINY AND INSATIABLE

No one has seen only one. I can assure you that he, who has seen one, has seen hundreds.

That is the way it is with the gnats known as the *mosquito Jején*. When they fall upon you, they are like a cloud of sharp darts.

The gnats are very small but are terrible blood suckers. They get so full that, unable to fly, they fall like tiny balls to the ground. That is why they are sometimes called rollers.

Once a gnat has bitten you, it leaves a small blood blister which later becomes a black dot.

Someone commented that fortunately the gnats are a daytime plague. When you are awake it is easier to defend yourself from such dreadful blood suckers.

Gnats are the terror of navigators traveling throughout the rivers of Amazonia since they are tiny and insatiable.

Gnats remind us of certain pleasures, which seem of no consequence, such as smoking a cigarette, drinking a couple of beers, or spreading gossip.

Little by little one discovers that they are small but unquenchable and continuously demanding without rest.

Fortunately, it is possible for us to follow St. Augustine's advice in order to free ourselves from those gnats that we carry within us:

"A bad habit when restrained gets deterred, when deterred it gets weaker and dies. And a bad habit is replaced by a good one."

SLANDER, SLANDER

N o more slander! It is not fair to pick on a poor creature.

We consider this creature to be violent, aggressive, a traitor, a delinquent, and a guilty assassin.

It has been the subject of novels, stories, and tales, and even reports from so called serious newspapers. In all accounts it is the villain.

I am referring to piranhas. Who said that piranhas are violent? There is not a river in the Amazon Basin without a few or perhaps even with many piranhas. If piranhas are as they say, how many swimmers, washerwomen, and fishermen would have already perished.

But no, the poor thing is only dangerous if it feels trapped or is isolated with its group in a lagoon where hunger causes it to grab whatever it sees moving. Then, I wonder if we would not act the same under similar conditions.

To preserve one's freedom or to save a life, would not a person perform actions that could be considered similar to piranha behavior?

Freedom, the same as life, is a priceless gift. Let St. Paul explain it better to you: "Freedom is what we have. Christ has set us free! Stand, then, as free people, and do not allow yourselves to become slaves again." (Galatians 5, 1)

MORTAL MIMICRY

The *Yaracara* or Jaracara snake is also called the four-nosed, rotten, and cat skin as well as many other names. It is highly poisonous and, as if this were not enough, its venom produces putrefaction of the flesh.

The Jaracara's high degree of danger, however, is mainly its excellent mimetic ability. It can take on the colors of dry leaves and the bark of certain trees.

Who knows why, to make things worse, the Jaracara is quite prolific.

Well, rabbits are also, so being prolific is not necessarily bad, but mimicry is deceitful. Mimicry may be deceiving to our vision, which can make us fall victim to our limited perceptions.

Confusing a little dry twig with a venomous snake is a terrible misfortune. We should be careful of this snake and other mimicry that surrounds us.

Yielding to mimicry is similar to becoming a wolf dressed in a sheep's skin.

St. John the Baptist dressed himself in an animal skin. When people confused him with Jesus, he avoided all mimicry. He declared "No, I'm not the Messiah" (John 1, 26). John was not seeking his own glory as happens when a person intentionally camouflages himself.

To this person, but also to all of us, St. Augustine's words fit well: "If you are obsessed with your own glory, how are you going to become seriously interested in the good of others?"

> *"To seek concrete solutions to the environmental crisis have proved ineffective, not only because of powerful opposition but also because of a more general lack of interest." (LS 14)*

PERICO LIGERO: THREE-TOED SLOTH

He who invented the name, *Perico ligero* (Fast Guy), must have been a master of the art of irony.

How did it occur to him to call this small creature, Fast Guy, since it moves so slowly that it is covered with algae?

Has anyone ever seen a slower mammal than this small sloth? Never!

No doubt, the three-toed sloth would completely agree with road signs that read: "Speed kills."

It is a strange nocturnal animal that moves by hanging from tree branches.

It holds on with its large, curved, and strong claws.

The sloth is covered with dense fur, originally gray, but, as mentioned above, it turns greenish when covered with algae. At least, the algae conceal the sloth from those seeking to do it harm.

Anyway, let us continue calling it, *Perico ligero* (Fast Guy). Perhaps this contrast can help us realize what we may become if someone praises us too much.

It is better to be a friend of the truth about oneself.

"The truth," writes St. Augustine, "is sometimes sweet and at other times bitter. But even when it is bitter, it produces health."

ALLIANCES OF LIFE

The jungle is not a paradise of tranquility. Here, life is a struggle and only the strongest, the most astute, or the one who knows how to establish the best alliances survives.

The passionflower is not an exception. It must struggle and orchestrate a few alliances.

Heliconia butterflies lay their eggs on the passionflower. So far, there is no problem. The trouble begins when the larvae are born with the appetite of a shark, and start feeding on the passionflower leaves.

The poor passionflower, not being foolish and in order to defend itself, produces and releases a toxic substance, cyanide.

However, instead of dying, the larvae assimilate the poison and mature into poisonous chrysalises and butterflies.

Thus the anxious passionflower has no choice other than to establish a special alliance with certain species of ants that eat the larvae. In this way the passionflower manages not to be completely eaten.

The passionflower establishes this alliance by generating pleasant nectars that attract ants. The ants also help keep butterflies from laying their eggs on the flower.

At the same time, the butterflies have the advantage of their inner poison to protect them from other predators.

Of course, other clever butterflies acquire the colors of Heliconia to show that they are poisonous, but they are not. This is the way they protect their own lives.

All alliances that favor life are welcome, from God's Great Alliance with humanity to the small alliances of the jungle.

"The replacement of virgin forest with plantations of trees, usually monocultures, is rarely adequately analyzed. Yet this can seriously compromise a biodiversity which the new species being introduced does not accommodate." (LS 39)

FATAL ANESTHESIA

People used to speak of two methods for extracting a tooth: with pain or without.

No need to tell you that the first one hurts more than the second.

The fact is that since anesthesia was invented, pain to humans has been mitigated considerably.

We should keep in mind that anesthesia can be beneficial but it can also be harmful.

The vampire bat or *chimbe* likes to feed on blood, as those who have seen a Dracula movie know.

The vampire bat is not a blood-sucker, as you may think, but simply a blood-licker. With its sharp teeth, the vampire bat makes a small incision by cutting a blood vessel, and then laps up the blood.

Some would say that one must be foolish to allow such a hideous creature to bite you and lick your blood.

What happens is that the vampire bat has the power to anesthetize its victims with its saliva or, as some believe, with the flapping of its wings. The fact is that the victim does not really feel the attack.

We find that anesthesia is not always used for good purposes. That of the vampire bat may prove to be fatal.

A different type of anesthesia which has spread in recent years is the loss of a sense of guilt or of a sense of sin.

Since the time when killing a human being was a grievous act, to the point of becoming a commonplace and easy act of getting even, a lot of anesthesia has passed under the bridge.

In order that this morally wrong anesthesia does not harm you, join St. Augustine in his prayer: "Lord, so that I do not grow insensitive to pain, grant me the grace to know how to cry."

POTBELLIED AND GOOD HEARTED

L et me clarify from the start that I am referring to a palm tree.

In order to elevate its lowly name which is not very flattering, it is fitting to remember that scientists in their high-sounding Latin call it *Dictocaryum plantysepalum*. But when translated back into simple terms, it again becomes potbellied palm.

Like all mortal things, the potbelly palm also decomposes.

And just when we believe that the palm deserves our disdain, not for being potbellied but for being rotten, it occurs that from the heart of the decaying palm a longed-for worm makes its appearance. This worm, known as the *arramojojoi* is a needed source of fat.

This worm is actually the palm's greatest value. In order to see its worth, you must overcome its appearance and go to its heart.

Fortunately, God proceeds in the same manner with you. He does not pay attention to your defects or iniquities. He goes deeper, and He knows how to find your worth in your heart.

I invite you to remember the anointment of David so that you can see that this is true. For Samuel, this process was a journey beyond appearances.

When Samuel first saw Eliab (David's older brother), he was impressed by his appearance. He thought that here was the one who should be anointed as king. But God said to Samuel:

Pay no attention to how tall and handsome he is. I have rejected him, because I do not judge as man judges. Man looks at the outward appearance, but I look at the heart. (1 Samuel 16, 7)

Venture to go beyond appearances and reach into the heart of others. Only the heart speaks to the heart.

FROM SALTY
TO SWEET

I am not adventuring into the appetizing world of culinary recipes.

Rather, I am delving into the almost whimsical world of some of the great transformations of Amazonia which have occurred through the passage of geological eras.

In one of those periods, called the Tertiary, we find that the Amazonia is part of the Pacific Ocean and separated from the Atlantic by the continental ridges of Brazil and Guiana, which at that time were joined together.

When the Andes Mountains rose at the end of the Cenozoic era an inland saltwater sea became separated from the Pacific Ocean.

Little by little, due to the abundant equatorial rains, the water of the sea lost its salinity and became a fresh or sweet water lake.

With the passing of centuries, this special lake began breaking through the barrier formed by the Guianan and Brazilian ridges and emptying into the Atlantic Ocean. It became the great Amazon River, a fresh water river with a variety of salt water fish such as dolphins, sharks, and rays.

It is not easy for anyone to be transformed into someone sweet when one has been bitter for so long. It takes time and, above all, letting oneself be inundated by the copious rains of the sweet water that falls from on High.

Let me share with you that, primarily, you must let yourself be inundated by the Water of Life that flows generously and which is called The Word of God.

THE UPWARD STRUGLE AND THE DOWNWARD STRUGGLE

ight, space, and food: These three elements cause most of the struggles in the jungle.

Who manages to survive in this world? Only those species which manage to adjust to the scarcity of light, space, and food or have the know-how to secure them.

When many species try to settle in the same place, the first thing that begins to dwindle is vital space in two dimensions: the horizontal and the vertical. It is necessary to struggle to conquer the ground space as both a physical support and as a source of food.

At the same time, it is necessary to struggle to clear an upward space in search for sunlight. Without light it is not possible to carry out the chlorophyllian function of the food production process.

In order to gain space and light, plants have developed innumerable and amazing anatomical and physiological strategies.

Sometimes the slender tops of young trees struggle to reach upward; at other times the roots configure themselves in such a way that they manage to conquer the space on the ground.

Without this double movement, upward and downward, nothing could survive.

Wherever they are on the earth, not even humans could subsist without these struggles. Human beings need both of these movements which can be described by two difficult words: immanence and transcendence.

Immanence is a downward struggle in order to maintain close contact with the world. Let us interpret this as a contact of love with the world of humans in which we live each day. Transcendence is our upward struggle in order to be in intimate communion with God. It is a continuous and endless struggle because love has no limit.

St Augustine expresses it in sublime words: "Thou hast made us for Thyself, O Lord, and our hearts are restless until they rest in Thee."

SYMBOLIC OR COMMERCIAL PERSPECTIVE

How should the resources of the jungle be managed?

If the answer comes from a colonist or newcomer, he would probably stress that the resources of the jungle must be managed with very clear commercial criteria where the economic productivity can be viewed.

If the answer comes from a native or indigenous person, he would stress that the resources of the jungle must be managed according to symbolic models and handled under the strict and well-known norms of shamans.

The results will tell us who is correct. If it is he who reduces everything to economic and commercial productivity, or if it is he who considers that the symbolic models are more important.

The indigenous people have learned to live in the rainforest without destroying it. The jungle is their ally, their friend, and a part of their cultural identity.

The colonist has found that the jungle is his enemy, his adversary, and it should be gotten rid of from its roots on up in order to profit commercially from the parcel of barren land that is left.

These are two different perspectives:

The one of the native who works in the jungle in order to live and the one of the colonist who lives in the jungle in order to work.

The mentality of the indigenous people for whom the jungle is an integral part of their culture differs from that of the newcomer who considers the jungle as something that you should enjoy in terms of an exploitation economy.

We could recall the verses of the Spanish poet Ramón de Campoamor:

In this treacherous world
Nothing is true or false;
Everything is according to the color
Of the crystal ball one looks through

Try to look through the crystal of Christ. You will be able to appreciate the wisdom of the natives who consider that man does not live by bread alone. You will also be able to understand the difficult situation of the newcomers who look to overcome poverty and also to have life in abundance.

FOREST WATER AND SEA WATER

The heavy downpour in Amazonia is awe-inspiring.

You might say that everyone should be drowned from the enormous amount of water that falls.

But, that is not the case. Even though it rains very often and in a torrential manner, the water knows how to divide itself so as to be beneficial and not harmful.

It so happens that 70% of the rain water remains in the canopy of the forest and only 30% falls to the ground.

The water that stays aloft serves as sustenance for the jungle then evaporates to fall again as another shower.

And if the forest did not exist, what would happen?

It's very simple. The water would end up in the sea, thus elevating its level.

This appears to be a simple matter and not very problematic. But don't tell that to the people of Holland who worry about an increase in sea level. Their country is located below sea level so any rise represents a serious danger to them.

May the forest canopy continue to receive 70% of the water for the benefit of the jungle and for all of the people. This is the wish of he who lives charity as it should be lived, on a planetary level, without frontiers, without walls of hatred, without divisions, while being a friend of all mankind, and not solely of my race, my town, or my nation.

You too may declare with St. Augustine:

I am a man
I live among men.
And nothing human
Is alien to me

"A rise in the sea level, for example, can create extremely serious situations, if we consider that a quarter of the world's population lives on the coast or nearby, and that the majority of our megacities are situated in coastal areas." (LS 24)

MAIL
SERVICE

Y ou need to make use of whatever is handy when necessity calls. This is the practice of the plants of Amazonia which require pollen to pass from one flower to another for their reproduction.

But the wind in Amazonia, officially in charge of this task, does not blow everywhere. Thus, plants must make use of an efficient mail service.

Flowers develop delightful fragrances, attractive colors, and delicious types of nectar in order to allure birds, insects, and bats. Enticed by such succulent dishes they search far and wide for flowers of the same species. Without intending to do so, they provide a very good mail service in order to transport the pollen.

I would be remiss at this moment if I did not introduce a bird that marvelously accomplishes this function and whose name is the hummingbird.

The hummingbird flies rapidly, it stands still in mid-air by beating its wings one hundred times per second, and if it has to flee it does so at 35 miles per hour.

To provide this service at such a great speed and we can only wish that our mail service would be this efficient, the hummingbird must eat with unbelievable frequency in order to compensate for its high energy use.

The following comparison is revealing: for his normal activity, a man needs 3,500 calories per day. If he performed an activity proportional to that of a hummingbird, he would have to consume no less than 155,000 calories per day.

This delightful bird is symbolic of the continuous wear and tear in the service for life and the vital task of this mail pollination in the jungle. The task of the hummingbird brings to mind those who serve life by facilitating encounters among people and between individuals and God, who is the very fountain of love and life.

How could I not call to mind the service of Christ: "I have come so that you may have life in its abundance." (John 10, 10)

> "God has written a precious book; whose letters are the multitudes of created things present in the universe… No creature is excluded from this manifestation of God: From panoramic vistas to the tiniest living form, nature is a constant source of wonder and awe. It is also a continuing revelation of the divine." (LS 85)

APPEARENCES ARE
DECEIVING

Medieval philosophers used to say that beauty and virtue go together.

It may be true, but the fact is that exceptions are not uncommon.

The strong, bright, and attractive colors among some reptiles of the jungle, instead of inviting you to approach them, are a warning that you are facing a dangerous animal.

Thus, the coral snake that elegantly dresses itself with those black and red rings has one of the deadliest toxic venoms.

There are some snakes in the jungle that must have read the fable of the donkey that put on a tiger's skin in order to frighten its enemies. These snakes also assume the colors of the coral snakes in order to confuse their predators.

This phenomenon of imitation, referred to as Batesian mimicry, can be a double-edged sword for these snakes. Often men kill the non-poisonous by confusing them with the authentic and dangerous coral snakes, but, after all, that is what the snakes wanted.

Definitely, beauty and virtue do not always go together. This is true in the case of the coral snake as well as the extremely poisonous frogs. They both are very poisonous and have beautiful colors. They can be found in Amazonia as well as other areas of the world.

There is another exception, that of the Pharisees of whom Jesus said, "You are like whitewashed tombs." (Matthew 23, 27-28)

THE OTHER HEN WITH THE GOLDEN EGGS

W hen the jungle is cleared some believe that a great treasure has been gained. Instead, the true treasure has been lost.

Here indeed, we actually re-tell the story of the hen who laid the golden eggs.

The jungle, with its enormous trees, animals, and abundance of vegetable species cannot live when the trees and undergrowth have been cut and burned.

The layer of humus in the Amazon is thin and fragile.

You merely have to observe a tree to discover that its roots do not penetrate very deeply but extend horizontally in order to stay within the very thin layer of humus.

Life actually comes from the canopy above. In each hectare of land, thirty tons of dead matter fall to the ground in a year. Thanks to the nutrient transformers, the debris then becomes food needed to continue life.

Clearing the jungle is to lose the hen and the golden eggs.

The story of this hen teaches you not to err in your search for treasure. You must procure a treasure that is not just of appearance but of true value.

Jesus warns you: "For where your treasure is, there will be your heart also." (Matthew 6, 21)

> "The ecosystems of tropical forests possess an enormously complex biodiversity which is almost impossible to appreciate fully, yet when these forests are burned down or levelled for purposes of cultivation, within the space of a few years countless species are lost and the areas frequently become arid wastelands." (LS 38)

OBSERVE THE BIRDS IN THE FOREST

Scientists tell us that the diversity of the tropical forest is amazing.

In an extension of about twenty-five acres they have discovered 1,500 species of flowering plants, 750 species of trees, 450 species of birds, 150 species of butterflies, 100 species of reptiles, 60 species of amphibians, and more than 8,000 different species of insects.

Let's admire two examples. The red-rumped cacique (*Cacicus*) is a very happy and boisterous bird that is capable of mimicking the singing of other birds and who enjoys living in very spirited groups.

The blue butterfly is a diurnal specimen with a beautiful metallic blue color. Its gentle and leisurely flight throughout the jungle and along the rivers is an unforgettable spectacle.

Truly, in the Amazon jungle one must follow Jesus's command to observe the birds of the forest, as well as, the reptiles, the butterflies, the amphibians, and the richness of the flora because they lead us to God.

"Ask the animals that swim in the water, those that dwell on the earth, and those that fly in the air. Ask of them all and they all will reply: 'Look at us, we are beautiful.' Their beauty is a confession. Who actually made that mutable beauty but He who is the immutable beauty?" (St. Augustine)

> "Many birds and insects which disappear due to synthetic agro toxins are helpful for agriculture: their disappearance will have to be compensated for by yet other techniques which may well prove harmful." (LS 34)

ALWAYS UPWARD

I t's the least they can do. Above all they must try to escape from the shadows. Stretch to the light. Climb as high as they can.

Such is the life of vines which are always programmed to reach for the sunlight.

They can become gigantic vegetable ropes with limbs twenty inches or more thick.

They very seldom climb the trunks of the big trees.

They seek their way towards the light by using the thin horizontal branches of young trees that are awaiting their turn to ascend to the canopy of the jungle.

There are many plants with their eager vines going upward toward the highest point so that they might be able to reach the light at its fullest.

Be a vine projected upward to the level of your aspirations and ideals in your quality of life and to the commitment of your faith.

It would not be bad to allow St. Paul to advise you:

Thus, then, if you have been resurrected with Christ, seek for things above, where Christ is seated at the right hand of God. Aspire to the things above, not to the ones on earth. (Col. 3, 1-2)

A FRIEND IS
A TREASURE

The Kayapó Indians speak about the "Ombigwa-o-tono" plant, which translated means "friends that grow up together."

They explain how some species develop with greater vigor when they are planted in union with specific varieties, while their growth is inhibited when they are associated with other species.

Such associations are described in terms of "plant energy."

The *Kayapó* are very skillful in associating the different energies and personalities of plants that show proof of productive yields.

This ability of the *Kayapó* makes us also aware that in the vegetable kingdom and not just in the human domain, a friend is a treasure.

And more so in the divine kingdom: "There is no greater friend than he who gives his life for his friends." Jesus expressed it with his words of wisdom and with his actions in life: "He had always loved those in the world who were his own, and he loved them to the very end." (John 13, 1)

THROUGH DEEP COURSES

I t looks to be so easy. The water seems to be so smooth and uniform, giving a person the impression of having at his disposal wide horizons upon which to navigate.

But that is not the case. The river is actually more deceiving than the broad jungles that beautifully appear along its banks.

River guides know this very well. They carefully observe the water since the river depths are not the same everywhere.

The motorists maneuver the boat in search of the secure path, that profundity which does not coincide with the whole of the river and often changes.

The deeper courses permit safe navigation. To go off the passageway is to run the risk that a canoe could end up crashing onto a sand bar barely covered by water.

Thus, in order to navigate successfully on the river, it is necessary to have three qualities:

To love the profound pathway as navigators and fisherman do.

To continuously look for a passageway which may not resemble a smooth paved road but which can change capriciously.

To accept being guided by a master of the waters who well knows how to distinguish the sound course.

When God chooses apostles, He also prefers those who have these three qualities.

LOOK FROM ABOVE OR YOU WILL SEE NOTHING

What a disappointment! He entered the jungle ready to face the most terrible dangers, to confront the most ferocious ophidians, and to discover the most exotic species of the Amazonian fauna.

After journeying miles and miles while carefully looking at trunks, plants, and holes, he saw nothing not even a blue butterfly.

He had thought that every fifteen feet he would be shadowed by a venomous serpent and monkeys would be taking turns to be caught by his camera!

"Where are they, he wondered sadly, where are the multiple species that everyone is talking about?"

Amazonia is indeed a habitat for multiple species but they cannot be discovered by looking at the humid forest at eye level.

They are mainly found in the forest canopy located above the jungle.

If you want to see something, you must look up. Perhaps it is better to say that one must look from above.

In order to clearly see God's works, we must also look from above.

DO NOT SHUT YOURSELF OFF: IT COULD BE BAD FOR YOU

No one could believe that the blue dress which was almost new and was kept with so much care inside the almost airtight armoire, so that any unpleasant insect would not touch it, has now turned white.

What happened? What went wrong in the art of wrapping?

Nothing failed. The wrapping was perfect. The dress was perfectly stored.

The awful thing that happened was precisely the hermetic sealing of the dress, because the humidity in the tropical forest is very high.

The more things are shut in or isolated from air and light, the more they become covered with a whitish or greenish fungus which appears due to the high level of humidity.

What is enclosed in a dark armoire is better left in the light where everyone can see it, and the sun's rays can hit it.

The humidity of the jungle invites you to be a friend of light and openness, and not sealed within an airtight environment.

Getting back to the blue dress, don't forget that the new garment in which you were clad on your baptismal day was indeed Christ.

You have been clothed with Christ but that vestment can also deteriorate if it is not exposed to the light of life, and if it is not manifested in the marvelous form of a clear testimony, made of love, service, and a joyful faith.

Don't leave your faith enclosed in the musty atmosphere of a private life.

NARROW HORIZONS, MALEVOLENT TORTURE

I ts small size doesn't keep it from challenging the deep cliffs, the enormous spaces, or the fast currents of the jungle river where it lives.

Once again the tiny turtle comes out with its small body of barely two inches to enjoy the sand bar and to happily walk on the infinite sand. The sun, so muted in the water, offers warmth to the extremities that slowly emerge from underneath its shell.

Suddenly, the turtle feels lifted.

It is a human hand that is gripping its shell and the tiny turtle suffers a great tumble.

These strange gyrations fill the turtle with fear.

When it is over, the turtle finds itself imprisoned inside a thing that we call a disposable cup.

There, in that strange world of narrow horizons, the only familiar thing is a couple of inches of water from the river which had never before set barriers on the turtle.

If you are a frog that lives in a well, all of this would appear to be normal. But if you are a frog that lives in the open river, you would feel anxiety.

If you have the heart of a mouse, all of this seems acceptable. If you have the heart of an eagle, you are terrified and cannot restrain your protest.

If you are a sectarian, all of this is normal. But if you are catholic, that is to say open to the universal and open to others without frontiers, all of this deserves your rejection.

Be catholic, all-inclusive, universal, without walls or frontiers, and with limitless love. Don't reduce yourself to the narrow horizons of the disposable cup of your individual worries and those strictly local concerns.

THOSE WHO ARE ABOUT
TO DIE SALUTE YOU

This phrase is well-known. Roman gladiators said it upon saluting their Cesar at the coliseum just before destroying each other in mortal combat.

"Those who are about to die salute you." This phrase came to me spontaneously when I read the list, not of human beings, but of those that we refer to as species on the way to extinction.

Who are those about to die that salute you?

The tapir of which only few remain, the curious armadillo of which Colombia has the largest in the world, the caiman which is harassed in order to become an exotic part of purses and shoes, the jaguar which is the largest feline in

America, the so shy and curious nutria, the ant eater, the river turtle, and many others.

Those who are about to die salute you. In their salute they are also asking: "Could you not do something for us so that we do not perish?"

A little bear, one of those on its way to extinction, was carrying a poster in his hand which said: "We want the children on their way to extinction to be able to live also."

The little bear was referring to those babies, who already conceived in their mother's womb, are also in danger of perishing.

Respond to the human solidarity of this little bear by allowing a spark of zoological solidarity within you while embracing his anxious call.

For the sake of the little bear and that of the babies!

"Because all creatures are connected, each must be cherished with love and respects, for all of us as living creatures are dependent on one another. Each area is responsible for the care of this family. This will require undertaking a careful inventory of the species which it hosts, with a view to developing programs and strategies of protection with particular care for safeguarding species heading towards extinction."
(LS 42)

THE NEW CRICKET

They are called arthropods and have a hard and not very elastic exoskeleton which keeps them from growing at the pace of their soft internal anatomy.

There are two possibilities for them: to remain scrawny or to abandon that rigid and narrow shelter.

They opt for the latter.

Speaking of one of the arthropods, the cricket abandons its old skeleton and acquires a new one which, little by little, takes shape to protect it.

Having an outside skeleton is an advantage for the cricket because at least it can liberate itself from the restrictive skeleton.

You also have an exoskeleton, the one which supports your entire spiritual structure.

The structure can become old and cause discomfort by enveloping you and hindering the freedom that you deserve.

But, as Paul assures, you can be born again and free yourself from the old person, as Jesus explained very well to Nicodemus.

Open up yourself to a new life. Pass from death to life and begin to grow to reach the stature of Christ.

THE RISKS OF LOVE

To fall in love is something quite risky. He who is in love is inclined to do anything to insure that he wins his loved one. Furthermore, love is an everyday risk and conquest.

Let the male frog, who must sing in order to attract his mate, show you in case you doubt me. He sings at full volume on moonlit nights.

The risk is not that the moon renders him more romantic on those special nights. The danger is that the frog-eating bat is around and has learned to recognize and locate the edible frog by his love song.

Therefore, the frog must be very careful on dark nights so that his love song does not call this dreadful bat, instead of his loved one.

The frog is cautious and knows how to take discreet measures. But he never abandons his love song.

Is it possible that love may lead him to the point of letting himself be devoured, to give up his life for his mate? Who knows?

But I do know of someone who did not doubt for an instant as he gave up his life for the benefit of his loved ones, and He explained it by saying that: "There is no greater love than one who gives up his life for his friends."

FORCED TO BE SOLITARY

Who doesn't enjoy being in good company? Even the mammals in the jungle like to be together in a herd.

But likes are one thing and needs are another.

In the jungle, with some exceptions, mammals are solitary animals. Said in more complex words, the density of individuals per square kilometer is extremely low.

The problem, simply speaking, is hunger. If they were all together, they would not find enough food for everyone.

That's why groups of mammals are very rare in the jungle.

Therefore, in times of hunger animals disperse themselves. If there were an abundance of food, they would probably stay together.

Human beings do the opposite.

In times of hunger people feel the need to gather together, to work collectively, and to join forces to undertake community enterprises.

Instead, when there is plenty each individual tends to ignore the other. People become more self-absorbed, self-sufficient, less sociable, less interested in the fortune of others, and thus more selfish.

Of course, there are also exceptions. That is why Jesus addresses spiritual hunger: "Blessed are the poor in spirit for theirs is the Kingdom of Heaven." (Matthew 5, 3)

GREEN PARADISE OR
RED DESERT

Have you heard of the great civilizations which were once famous such as the Mayans, the Egyptians, and the Babylonians?

Do you know what happened to these renowned civilizations?

They were devoured by the desert.

I don't need to tell you how it came about. If you could only see what's happening in Amazonia today, you would realize how it's possible to disappear by being devoured by the desert.

In the area of tropical forests, the evaporation level of water surpasses 1,400cc per year, which is a great quantity of water. While in the drier prairie areas the evaporation level only reaches 1,000cc per year, which indicates that there is much less water evaporating.

If the water loss continues at this rate, we'll find ourselves in an arid zone. Will Amazonia perhaps shift from being a green paradise to becoming a red desert? We still have time so it may not happen.

Speaking of a green paradise or a red desert, don't forget that your heart can also become an arid zone. Thus when the farmer comes to plant his seeds, they will fall on sterile ground.

Prepare your soil to allow the seed to fall on good earth so that the yield may be a hundred-fold. Then you will also become a green paradise.

"One particularly serious problem is the quality of water available to the poor. Every day, unsafe water results in many deaths and the spread of water-related diseases, including those caused by microorganisms and chemical substances." (LS 29)

TOO MANY, USELESS, AND HARMFUL

These adjectives could be added to a thousand more. All of them negative in mood and uttered in a disgusting tone.

Who are these creatures so disliked, useless, and harmful? They are simply insects.

But, what a surprise! If you go to Amazonia, you will find that there are no useless insects. All insects are in some way beneficial to man.

The sting of ants and wasps injects a substance that cures at least twelve different diseases.

Termites transform wood into fertile soil and from this soil people obtain food and nourishment. Almost all fish feed on insects and we know that fish make good food.

Many flowers are beautiful because they want to attract insects.

John the Baptist used to eat locust, we don't know if he ate them fried or simply raw. Many indigenous people eat locust, and they as well as others find ants and other insects to be exquisite dishes.

The truth is that each living being is useful for something.

Look at those persons who you see as unbearable and think of as useless. Search for their usefulness and their beautiful contribution to the whole of humanity.

You will begin to appreciate them much more than you do insects.

Let's consider a question: Do you think of yourself as an insect? Somewhat like the man in Kafka's dream who woke up as an insect?

Discover your own usefulness. You are good for many things. God has given you a mission and the qualities to accomplish it. Don't lose sight of your mission.

Don't say what Jeremiah said: "Lord, I am only an insect." You will receive the very same answer that he was given: A great mission was entrusted to him, the mission of a prophet with the certainty that God would always be with him.

"In assessing the environmental impact of any project, concern is usually shown for its effects on soil, water and air, yet few careful studies are made of its impact on biodiversity, as if the loss of species or animals and plant groups were of little importance." (LS 35)

TWO PATHS OF SALVATION

I do not know if it is the specialty of the best restaurants or of the worst restaurants. It could be of the best since its meat is of excellent quality. It could be of the worst since the hunting and consuming of it is forbidden.

And because it is such a tasty dish, the poor little animal has to think of a thousand ways to save itself.

It is the *Boruga* or the Lowland Paca, and it often digs very intricate caves as a means of defense. The unique aspect of these caves is that they have both land and water outlets since they are constructed near rivers and lakes.

At sundown, the paca goes out to the riverbank in search of food which consists of herbs and fruits. But there too is the jaguar that stalks it, the ocelot that chases it, or the man who aims his weapon at it. At the least sign of danger, the paca rushes into the cave. And if the trained hunting dogs insist on getting the paca out of its refuge, it uses one of those two outlets, either water or land, for its salvation.

I will not deny that I would like to see you converted into a paca. I don't say this so that you must face the dangers that besiege this small creature.

May you be like a paca and learn how to use the two ways of salvation that God offers you. Passage by water, that magnificent sign of salvation, should remind you of the Passover which you experience through the Word and the Sacraments. Passage by land (humus) that is a term suggesting homo or man which is the other path to salvation.

The first passage through water was used by Moses as a child and that is why he is referred to as "He who was saved by the water," and later as an adult, Moses crossed the liberating Red Sea. This was a foreshadowing of the Passover, the veritable passing from slavery to liberation or from death to life.

The second route was used by the Good Samaritan when he chose as his path of salvation to assist the assaulted man who was wounded and half-dead.

Jesus said: "I was sick and you visited me, come into the Glory of your Lord."

Be a "paca." Bring together these two truths of salvation, that of water which faith demands of you and that of land which love asks of you.

STRATIFICATION

The struggle is due to the following: the city is divided into strata. A stratum is a horizontal division of a society, such as the different layers of the earth.

The most luxurious neighborhoods and buildings are located on the sixth stratum and, of course, they pay more taxes. Those on the fourth stratum pay less and those on the first and second pay almost nothing.

The struggle begins when those on the sixth stratum want to pay taxes as if they were on the fourth stratum or if those on the second stratum get a tremendous bill as though they were on the sixth stratum.

At this moment I am not really interested in this type of human struggle.

Instead I want to talk about stratification in the jungle. You may find it hard to believe, but there are strata there as well.

As in the city, jungle inhabitants are also stratified. I am not referring to birds or other animals.

I am only referring to mammals such as monkeys, from the mottled-face tamarind to the tufted capuchin. They are at the highest rank and would be at the fourth level. Obviously those who live at this highest level are in the tree tops.

The next lower or third rank is shared by two groups: the runners and the climbers.

I would be remiss if I didn't mention that this rank is occupied by the jaguar, puma, and ocelot.

Down to the second rank are those animals whose lives are rather subterranean. It includes many types of rodents, a variety of armadillos, as well as the much-sought after lapa or paca.

While at the lowest or first rank we find mammals that dwell near water including the tapir, capybara, otter, and nutria.

Stratification, as you see, seems to be inevitable in both people and animals.

Best of all, and this applies personally, you are also stratified in your inner self.

Leave the world of the jungle for a moment and examine the world of values.

There are the higher values such as the great ideals for which you are ready to abide and to sacrifice yourself. Those rank as superior values.

Then there are those less high values for which you also sacrifice, but without considering them as superior ranking.

Finally, we have values that are good and by which you are willing to abide, but in a moment of value conflict you may prefer to set them aside in order to preserve those superior values.

Don't permit a greater value to slip unconsciously to the last stratum. Don't permit secondary values to replace or take over, in a sort of a spiritual coup d'état, those of the superior stratum.

If this were to happen, I hope you may be overcome by a crisis.

This crisis results in the purification, reorganization, and repositioning of each value to its rightful place. This process can be referred to as a conversion.

Don't fail to look at Jesus and his Gospel when you set in motion the task of reorganizing your values according to a sound, human, and Christian stratification.

TIMES OF REVOLUTION

N ot long ago another centennial of the French Revolution was celebrated.

The truth is that despite significant accomplishments many felt shame instead of pride about this revolution that took place near the end of the Eighteenth Century.

And this is understandable. The revolution came to be an absurd time of killing in which people of all social and political conditions fell as victims.

A question was asked of someone who lived through those days: "What did you do during the revolution"?

"Me, I lived!" the person responded. "Was that not enough?"

This was quite an accomplishment in those revolutionary times.

But it's no less of an accomplishment today, when we seem to live in an anti-ecological revolution.

If a South American coati meets a capybara and asks: "What are you doing during this revolution? The capybara may reply: "I live. Is that not enough?"

Of course this is no small accomplishment.

If the question is asked of the human spirit which is open to the transcendence of God in these times of secular revolution and latent opposition to religious values.

What do you do during this revolution?

The human spirit may rightly answer: "I live. Is that not enough?"

Long live life, all forms of life, from the life of the harassed capybara to our own eternal life which is the greatest aspiration of a Christian.

Down with this revolution against life!

> *"We see increasing sensitivity to the environment and the need to protect nature, along with a growing concern, both genuine and distressing, for what is happening to our planet." (LS 19)*

HAVING THE DEPTHS AT HAND

Traveling along the enormous rivers of the Amazon basin, it is possible to admire large numbers of turtles receiving the abundant tropical warmth. They may be laying in a row on a trunk that has fallen into the river or perhaps immobile on the sandy beaches.

What expression do they have? Is it of satisfaction or sleepiness or of joy?

Who knows? The fact is that when you try to get closer than you should, the turtles immediately plunge into the water. After all, they do have great depths at hand.

This event does not have much transcendence. One time, a comparable situation happened to St. John of the Cross that great Mystic and Doctor of the Church.

A humble nun, in the simplicity of her life in a convent, asked him a childlike question:

"Why, my father, when I go near the pool of water in the orchard, the frogs on the edge jump into the water and sink to the bottom as soon as they hear the noise of my steps?"

"The frogs jump into the water because there they have security and protection. You should do the same. When you see tribulation approaching, plunge in with God and there you will be safe and tranquil and no one can do you harm."

The same truth is proclaimed in Psalm 90: "Lord, you have been our refuge through the ages."

COMPANIONSHIP

I n the tropical lowlands it never snows. This is a known fact.

But, it is undeniable that you can see trees that look as though an enormous mass of snow has fallen on them.

During certain times of the year many white herons make their appearance. At the setting of the sun, they choose a single tree in which to spend the night in pleasant companionship.

We can also see beautiful birds from a different family gathering in another tree to spend the night. The beauty of this phenomenon is the inclination to keep company with those with whom you have an affinity.

From the habits of these birds we can observe the companionship of Faith.

With one Lord, one Faith, and one baptism the Church is one body united. This is what we call the companionship of Faith.

A heron alone at night is inconceivable. The same goes for a solitary Christian. To be a Christian is to be part of a family, a community of faith, or an assembly of affinity.

The Fathers of the Church used to say that, with the companionship of the faithful, a Christian is not alone.

I advise you to seek, accept, encourage, and live this companionship of Faith. This is suggested by the beautiful herons of Amazonia.

EXTERIOR DIVESTING, INTERIOR SOLIDITY

They are labeled transporters and also defoliators. This second name well fits this group of ants. With their skillful jaws, they cut pieces of green leaves from trees and take them to their nests.

They don't feast on the leaves; they simply store them inside their anthill. The ants grow fungi on the leaves which they use as their main food.

Their cutting actions may appear to be cruel especially upon seeing a poor tree stripped of many of its green and fresh leaves.

That is not the case, and things are not that tragic. On the one hand, the leaf-cutting ants often change trees. On the other hand, the most special benefit is that the material that the ants carry becomes waste which is rich in hydrogen, phosphates, magnesium and calcium. Other plants will absorb this material through their roots to increase their vitality.

Thus the exterior stripping is transformed into an interior solidity. It is a process that we can call higher formation. This procedure brings to mind the image of great teachers of spiritual life. They insist on divesting exteriorly in order to increase one's interior solidity.

They demand from a novice of spiritual life the estrangement, renouncement, and distancing from that which is secondary in order to clear space for the acquisition of inner strength. They ask the novice to strip off their leaves in order to fortify their roots and trunk.

As St. Augustine, the great Saint and Doctor of the Church would say about the exterior divesting and interior solidity in terms of love: "The greatest enemy of love is many loves." Therefore, in order to fill oneself, one must empty oneself. As the great reformer and poet, St. John of the Cross, would say in beautiful rhymes from his *Spiritual Canticle*, XXVIII:

My soul is occupied,
And all my substance in His service;
Now I guard no flock,
Nor have I any other employment:
My sole occupation is love.

EFECTIVE SENTINELS

entries, night watchmen, supervisors, guards, sentinels, and patrolmen are very common jobs in our insecure society.

And this is not without a reason with such a desire for easy, fast, and abundant profits.

But this need of protection is not only in a civilized society.

In the jungle there is also a need to contract for this type of workforce.

Certain tropical plants have made contracts with insect-eater (Bullet) ants for vigilance and patrolling. These ants clear the surface of plants where other insects have deposited their eggs and larvae.

They also defend the plant against other enemies such as herbivorous animals. And, of course, they defend the plant from people. He who touches, even without malice, a plant or a trunk that is patrolled by these Bullet ants, will soon realize that they are determined, efficient, and very painful.

When it comes to being an effective sentinel there is no reason to not be alert and energetic.

Didn't the foolish virgins lack energy when they were supposed to watch for the husband's arrival and when he arrived they were not there?

And talking about the Bullet ants, I recommend that you keep in your heart one tiny Bullet ant for special cases, like Peter the Apostle tells us: "Be alert, be on watch! Your enemy, the Devil, roams around like a roaring lion, looking for someone to devour. Be firm in your faith and resist him." (1 Peter 5, 8)

EACH ONE OCCUPIES ITS SPACE

Let us go back to the theme of stratification. Mammals are not the only ones who organize themselves into different strata, birds that fly all over the place are also stratified. At the fourth level of stratification which is above the canopy are those birds that soar to the heights and have powerful vision such as eagles and sparrow hawks.

Dropping down to the third level of stratification which is at the peak of the forest canopy, we find curious birds such as the toucans with their enormous beaks, talkative parrots, and beautiful hummingbirds.

At the second level of stratification which is in the middle of the forest, we see woodpeckers, quetzals, blue-crowned motmots or "pájaros bobos", and Ruddy wood-creepers.

Concluding our descent to the first level of stratification there is an abundance of hermit hummingbirds, flycatcher birds, ant-shrike birds, curassow birds, the *pavas* or fowl-like birds, and various species of wrens.

The truth is that each bird occupies its own space. The wren does not roam in the zone of the harpy, that sizeable and ferocious eagle, nor would the sparrow hawk like to live among the low bushes like a simple water duck.

This is a natural stratification where, perhaps, life's security dictates its own laws. Also in other realms, especially that of human beings, each occupies their own space.

Curiously, St Augustine would say that in the Amazon jungle the place of each is determined not as much for their security, as by their body weight:

Each by its body weight tends to occupy its proper place. It is not necessarily going down, but being at its own place. Fire tends to go up; a stone tends to go down. Oil poured on water elevates itself on top of the water. Water poured over oil settles beneath the oil. They settle to their own place according to their weight. That which is not at its own place becomes restless. If you put it in its own place, it rests.

My weight is my love: by it I am carried wheresoever I am carried... God's love inflates and elevates us. We ascend in our heart and sing the song of the upward steps. Inflamed with the fire of the love of God we climb upward on the path that leads us to peace. (*Confessions*, 3. 9. 10)

LET THEM GO SOMEPLACE ELSE!

I t is so easy to set fire to the forest and then to ease your conscience by saying of the animals and even the people: Let them go someplace else!

Instead, is it somewhat difficult to understand the phenomenon called endemism? That is, the narrow geographical distribution of species and their essential dependency on their habitat.

Every time a creature is taken out of the jungle, the comment of people of the local community is usually: "This one is going to die."

This phrase, expressed with concern or with indifference, shows the profound link between the life of an animal and the Amazon area in which it lives. The infringement of this linkage means torture and death.

Let them go someplace else! This sentence is shouted to the indigenous people of Brazil and other places where oil, mining, or the lumber industry become more valuable than human beings. People are drawn to their land, not by the interest of economic production, but by profound emotional, cultural, and historical ties.

The exiled people of Israel gave an emotional account of their separation from their land:

> By the rivers of Babylon
> We sat down;
> There we wept when we remember Zion.
> On the willows near by
> We hung up our harps.
>
> Those who captured us told us to sing;
> They told us to entertain them:
> "Sing us a song about Zion."
>
> How can we sing a song to the Lord in a foreign land?
> May I never be able to sing again
> If I forget you, Jerusalem! (Psalm 137)

> *"The human environment and the natural environment deteriorate together; we cannot adequately combat environmental degradation unless we attend to causes related to human and social degradation. In fact, the deterioration of the environment and of society affects the most vulnerable people on the planet." (SL 48)*

MODERN
MORAL
MIMICRY

Typical of the jungle, mimicry serves to mislead many. The insect that turns into a twig goes unnoticed. The snake that takes on the appearance of an innocent vine makes it easy for the victim to come close enough for the snake to catch it.

Mimicry in the jungle is not an exclusive feature of wild animals. One of the wildest things to happen in the jungle is not caused by animals. It is fierce capitalism which traps its victims by means of a modern moral mimicry.

Market forces are perhaps the most serious menace to the tropical rainforests. Since priority is given to immediate profits, these market forces often push out entire communities.

As always, the newcomer (*colono*) is accused of the depredation and destruction of ecosystems. There are reasons to blame him, and it is easy to accuse him since he does not use mimicry.

Instead, oil, lumber, and mining companies declare themselves absolved of all wrongdoing. How do they do it? Very easily! A type of modern mimicry enters into play, a mimicry that we have called moral since that is its nature, but, obviously, it is immoral, since that is its condition.

They seek to gain their innocence by presenting themselves as creators of much needed sources of work, as the driving force of indispensable development, and as the true discoverers of national wealth. Thus, the confirmed ecological issues have developed into a very serious moral problem.

For many thousands of years, man lived simply and passively through the slow natural evolution of the cosmos. But the moment arrived when humans become nature's protagonist. At first the few modifications that man introduced were minor. Gradually, the changes reached a major level. At that moment, morality came into play. In addition to hurting each other in war, men damage the world's natural base under the false pretext of wanting to serve humanity.

This so-called service to humanity should be renamed as modern immoral mimicry. It is an appropriate label that covers the damage caused to nature for present and future generations. Jesus spoke of "whitewashed tombs." (Matthew 23, 27)

> *"To seek concrete solutions to the environmental crisis have proved ineffective, not only because of powerful opposition but also because of a more general lack of interest." (LS 14)*

A GUIDE FOR
FORMICARIIDAE

That's the way it is. They are called *formicariidae*, which is a difficult name to understand and pronounce. Maybe it would be easier if we just remembered that *formiciidae* refers to ants.

Since these animals are named after ants and they live by hunting and eating ants we mustn't confuse them with just any old ant-eater.

If they have something to do with ants it is that they like to watch for ants, especially during an active period when army ants launch their marches.

When their march progresses to within a few meters of the vanguard the army ants produce such an alarm among other insects that they all start moving around crazily, abandoning their refuges, and trying to escape. Then the *formicariidae* or antbird of the passerine bird family takes advantage of this moment of panic to catch and eat as many ants and other insects as possible.

Furthermore, the antbird appears to be good hearted since when it discovers the marching ants it immediately calls to other antbirds to join the feast.

Do the ants know the immense favor that they do for the antbird? And, is the antbird grateful with the favor the army ants do for it?

The army ants with their life and movement are the living arrows that show the antbird where the fields of abundant food are to be found.

They are like Moses who knew where to lead his thirsty people to fountains of fresh water.

They could be compared to the Star of Bethlehem which led the Wise Men to the crib of the Savior of the World.

They are like genuine Christians, who, with their lives, actions, and words, show the path that leads to Jesus Christ the fountain of eternal life.

AMAZONIA'S COCA AND THE FIVE "F'S"

"No to coca, yes to rubber." This is the slogan of a campaign among a group of immigrants in the region. The campaign is encouraged and administered by a parish in the Colombian Amazonia (Remolino-Caquetá).

The campaign has been successful. In their fields the newcomers have planted a total of 1,000 hectares (2,500 acres) of rubber trees. The only problem is that nearby, there are still other 90,000 hectares (225,000 acres) of coca plants. And, coca is not simply a product which is forbidden, but also a phenomenon that impacts the biological, cultural, social, and religious elements of the Amazonian environment.

There are five affected Amazonian elements whose names begin with the letter "F". The damage to these five elements is aggravated by the malignant coca phenomenon:

Flora   Fauna
Fraternity   Family
Faith

Flora: The regrettable destruction of the flora in Amazonia is made worse by a lack of scientific knowledge concerning the life of many of the species.

Fauna: The habitat loss each day causes the list of endangered species to grow. This includes many species, such as insects, of which we have limited knowledge.

Fraternity: Fraternity among the people is blemished by mafia violence. This viciousness is responsible for outbreaks of vengeance, unsettled disputes, dissolute life styles, and placing the value of making fast, easy, and abundant money above even the life of their fellow man.

Family: Family ties in the conditions of the jungle are very fragile. More so because of the presence of a large migrant population who arrives in such a transient mode that they even establish temporary marriage unions.

Faith: Faith as obedience to the Lord's Gospel becomes shattered when it is turned into a simple lucky charm in order to help guarantee high profits from illicit investments. This "drug-conscience" phenomenon has led to the destruction of the social, communal, and cultural fabric of Amazonia. To save Amazonia from this ruin is to save these five affected elements: Flora, Fauna, Fraternity, Family, and Faith.

Either, they are saved together or they perish together.

THE TEN
PLAGUES OF
AMAZONIA

I t did not happen solely in Egypt. There, of course, the apprehension was great when the Egyptian population saw itself being beaten by the ten plagues by which the God of the Hebrews wanted to force their Pharaoh to let His people go.

Plagues have also been the terror of farmers.

But now, let's talk about another ten plagues which aren't solely the terror of farmers but of the tropical rainforest called Amazonia.

1. **Deforestation:** This is the slashing and burning of the forest, a system practiced by the colonists and also by large lumber, mining, and oil companies.

2. **Extinction:** This is the loss of genetic diversity as well as diversity of species due to the destruction of their habitat.

3. **Erosion:** Because of the hard beating of rainwater on the deforested land, the soil becomes barren and loses vegetable life.

4. **Degradation:** This is the damage suffered by the soil due to several factors. One is the compacting of the soil caused by excessive cattle farming and another is the relocation of clay and sand which triggers floods, diminishing of fish, and other ills.

5. **Pollution:** One of the main sources of contamination comes from the waste that is released into the water by the multitude of cocaine laboratories functioning in Amazonia.

6. **Latifundia:** These are large-landed estates that are constantly growing due to extensive cattle farming. This brings about more lands being placed in the hands of fewer owners.

7. **Exclusion:** The dynamics of the social organization of Amazonia has originated zones of exclusion. Here the constructive presence of the government has been marginal or almost nil. The victims of exclusion zones have been the indigenous people and new immigrants.

8. **Internal and external violence:** Harsh living conditions, lack of resources and education, and conflicts with *guerrillas* and drug traffickers generate a high level of internal violence. We must also add the external violence which comes from companies seeking fat profits within a short period of time.

9. **Inoperativeness:** In order to save Amazonia, a set of responses must come from the national government and the local communities. A multiplicity of ecological laws has been created, but they have remained mostly on paper. Their application has not been achieved due to various interferences and contradictions.

10. **Ecological Ignorance:** Lack of knowledge is not exclusively of the colonists, but also of some governmental bureaucracies. There is a lack of understanding of the realities of the region and unawareness of the true value of this tropical rainforest.

These are ten plagues that may require international cooperation and changes in economic structures in order to save Amazonia.

"There has been a tragic rise in the number of migrants seeking to flee from the growing poverty caused by environmental degradation. They are not recognized by international conventions as refugees; they bear the loss of the lives they have left behind, without enjoying any legal protection whatsoever. Sadly, there is widespread indifference to such suffering, which is even now taking place throughout our world." (LS 26)

THE BITTER TRUTH OF A SWEET LIE

There are falsehoods that have been taken as truths for many centuries or at least for many years. One of these untruths concerns the Amazon jungle and it is expressed in the well-known and many times repeated phrase: "The Amazon Jungle is the lungs of the world."

We are overwhelmed and almost asphyxiated with worry when we realize this enormous source of oxygen is undergoing destruction.

The destruction is indeed true, real, dramatic, and regrettable. What is not true is that Amazonia is the lungs of the world in the sense stated above.

Scientists tell us that, given its condition as a mature forest, the Amazon jungle is not exactly an oxygen producer, but instead, its function may be defined as one of balancing between the production and absorption of oxygen.

The image is inappropriate. As we know, lungs do not produce oxygen. Instead, they take it from the atmosphere and release it transformed into carbon dioxide.

But then, this misconception about the Amazon Jungle being the lungs of the world becomes a truth that unfortunately is more bitter than sweet.

The destruction of the forest caused by burning is indeed transforming Amazonia into the lungs of the world, given that the combustion of wood evidently causes liberation of large quantities of carbon dioxide that have adverse effects upon the climatic conditions of the world.

The major effect, as we know, is global warming which occurs as a consequence of the phenomenon identified as the "greenhouse effect."

Of all of the gases that impact global warming through the greenhouse effect, the one that contributes the most (58%) is specifically carbon dioxide (CO_2).

Therefore, the new Catechism of the Catholic Church did not fail to include an ecological warning:

"The dominion granted by the Creator over the mineral, vegetable, and animal resources of the universe cannot be separated from respect for moral obligations, including those toward generations to come." (354)

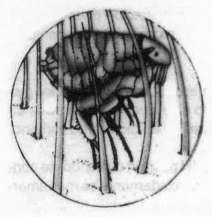

A PLEASANT DECEIT

I t is so tiny that you are unable to avoid it. Instead it ends up burrowing under your skin and invading your body

I am speaking of the *chigoe* flea or chigger.

Has anyone seen a *chigoe* in action? Perhaps, no one has.

It gently burrows under the skin and this action produces a slight burning sensation that can be described as pleasant.

Just like the pleasurable sleepiness that one feels when the effects of the malaria virus begin, the *chigoe* also ingratiates itself to its victim.

The deceit begins cloaked in pleasure.

The *chigoe's* infection is just like the terrible effects of malaria in that it begins with an agreeable deception from which you find it difficult to defend yourself.

In both cases, that which begins well ends badly.

Even less so if you are accustomed to identifying that which is agreeable with good and that which is disagreeable with bad.

This identification is natural in children. That is why this conditioning in terms of pleasure instead of pain works well with them.

But when childhood ends, the mature person must reach the understanding that not everything pleasant is good nor is everything unpleasant bad.

Pleasure, like temptation, can lead you to perdition. The disagreeable, like martyrdom, may lead you to excel. Consider the struggle of St. Augustine while trying to overcome the identification of good with always being agreeable:

And the sorrow of the century, as happens in our sleep, weighted sweetly upon me. And the thoughts that were taking me to You were like the attempts of someone trying to awaken and then falling back to sleep while being defeated by the pleasurable state of drowsiness…

I repeated unhurried and sleepy words to myself: 'now,' 'in a minute,' 'just a little longer.' But the 'now' never ended and the 'in a minute' was taking a long time.

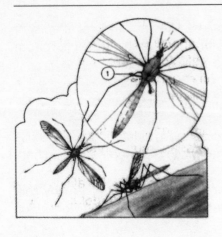

MY PLACE
OF REFUGE

Malaria! Terror of Amazonia!

How we wish for the prompt development of an effective vaccine. Meanwhile, let's continue trying to defend ourselves from this terrible mosquito, the Anopheles.

At six o'clock in the evening it makes its appearance. A member of a little-known family of insects, Anopheles is one of the true beasts of the jungle.

If you are distracted, it will get you. If you fall asleep, it will take advantage of you.

Either way it can produce endless anguish.

This anguish ends when you manage to get inside the mosquito net which covers your entire bed, provided that the hateful insect is not able to get inside.

The mosquito net is a fabulous invention to enable sleep! Simple and yet reliable, the net offers you safe protection; it gives you tranquility; it restores your serenity; it becomes a solid shield against all attacks.

Oh, what an evoking symbol of God is the mosquito net!

He, who saved Daniel in the pit of lions (Daniel 6, 22) and He who protected David from falling into the hands of Saul was praised by David as a divine net:

> The Lord is my protector;
> He is my strong fortress.
> My God is my protection
> And with Him I am safe.
> He protects me like a shield;
> He defends me and keeps me safe.
> He is my savior;
> He protects me and saves me from violence.
> I call to the Lord, and He saves
> Me from my enemies.
> Praise the Lord! (2 Samuel 22, 2-4)

"The violence present in our hearts, wounded by sin, is also reflected in the symptoms of sicknesses evident in the soil, in the water, in the air and all forms of life." (LS 2)

"The earth herself, burden and laid waste, is among the most abandoned and maltreated of our poor; she 'groans in travail' (Rom 8:22)." (LS 2)

LOWER YOUR HEAD A BIT
OR YOU MAY SINK

ot even a needle would fit inside. The speedy glide boat, full as it was, was ready to begin a long trip on this river basin in Amazonia.

As usual, the boat took off fast and secure.

But in a few seconds everyone noticed that the bow of the boat was too high. The excessive weight in the rear kept the bow from being lowered while the stern, already level with the water line, soon would be flooded.

All of the passengers feared the worst. Someone began to protest that the boat was overloaded with cargo (obviously, someone else's cargo).

Another recalled how poorly he was able to swim, even though more than once he could have learned.

Well, everyone hoped that the bow of the risky boat would drop a little so that they would not end up wet or drowned.

This simple boat can teach many things. When it is loaded to excess, it becomes the faithful reflection of a person who is so full of himself that he does not have that tiny bit of humility which will allow him to lower his head a little.

If you are one of those persons who are filled to the brim with pride, be careful that you do not plummet into the depths. Lower your head a little bit in order to avoid sinking.

Counter pride with humility.

A MASTER OF THE CURRENT, NOT ITS SLAVE

In Spanish we sometimes ask, "Where does Vincent go?" The answer is, "Where everyone goes."

This is just a saying. It is used to describe the mind of a person who always lets others pull him along, who lets others dominate him, and who does not know how to walk on his own two feet in a direction chosen by him.

This happens among human beings, but it doesn't occur among the swift boats or canoes that traverse rivers.

A boat always has a rope tied to the front and an oar extended along the side. These are the tools that are used to struggle against the strong and, at times, treacherous river current.

When you stop the motor, the current wants to take over and pull the boat along.

This is not a problem if it has a rope and an oar. It tells the current: "I am going where I should and not where you pull me."

Do not forget to carry the rope of a well-defined personality with you every moment of your life. One that does not let the current drag you but knows well where you should go.

And, do not forget the oar of a right decision which leads you to choose the correct way and not where others want to push you.

To those who followed the currents in vogue in the religious sphere, thus becoming unfaithful to their faith and its principles, St Augustine would tell them: "You run very well but down the wrong road."

Do not let yourself be dragged by the thousands of currents that seek to manipulate you. Do not let others say that you navigate very well, but down the wrong river.

ELEVATE YOURSELF A LITTLE MORE

T he very thin legs identified it as a member of the heron species, but without any doubt not one of the most illustrious.

Actually, its plumage was not elegant. It was the brownish-gray color of a timeworn mouse. That ugly bird only came to our attention by the fact that it was standing aloof in the middle of the road.

The noise of our vehicle alerted it. The bird immediately took impetus and soared into the heights.

How beautiful! A resplendent white color appeared from underneath its wings in a wonderful contrast to its now brilliant black upper tone. This gave its flight an air of great solemnity.

What a mistake to think that this was an ugly bird. It was truly a beautiful, worthy, and appealing bird.

This is what it means to soar to the heights and to elevate the level of your own aspirations. This is what happens when you make the decision to place yourself above the dusty ground.

Then the beautiful, the treasured, and the appealing qualities come into view.

Paul was right to invite you to seek and taste the glorious heights and not to remain down in the imperfect dust of the earth.

Elevate yourself a little more. Soar to the heights. Hidden virtues will wonderfully shine as well as other magnificent qualities now obscured by the dust.

AS PRUDENT AS SERPENTS

Neither courage nor pity! These two virtues disappeared like magic.

It happened when I was about to enter my office; a serpent slowly slithered down the tiled corridor. Someone, moved by ecological sentiments, exclaimed: "We should let it go!" With not a bit of pity and with my thumb down in Nero's fashion, I replied: "Kill it!" My response implied, obviously, that I was not going to be the executioner. Why not? It was simply because of my lack of courage.

In a monthly publication, someone wondered: "Why do we hate them so much?" It is actually a case of fear for what they can do to us. *Apodals*, having no feet or limbs, are swift and silent creatures with sharp fangs that can take your life away with a single bite. Many people die in Amazonia each year from the lethal venom of an ophidian. All together 30,000 people die in the world as a result of a serpent's bite. India is in first place and it is followed by Amazonia and the other humid forests of South America.

Their venom is composed of either neurotoxins or enzymes. The former affects the nervous system and can paralyze breathing. The latter, slower and crueler, can destroy the blood by either liquefying or coagulating it, and it can also affect the liver and kidneys. For our own peace of mind, it is good to add two points. First, serpents don't have any intention of attacking human beings, and more often than not they hide from us. Accidents do occur when the reptile is startled or feels cornered with no escape. Second, even with their bad reputation, they still prefer to go unnoticed.

Many people who have visited Amazonia say that they have not seen even a single snake! If people really knew how close they had been to a serpent, and more than once, they would have done triple somersaults out of pure panic; but they didn't see anything, and what the eye doesn't see, the heart doesn't dread.

This all shows that serpents prefer the prudence of remaining hidden more than in infusing terror. So, the serpents' prudence can render us a major benefit.

Perhaps now you understand a little more of what Jesus meant when He told us to be as prudent as serpents.

Learn to keep your place without attempts at false prominence, by simply being upright and avoiding evil through the prudence which Jesus tries to teach you when He illustrates a special profile of serpents.

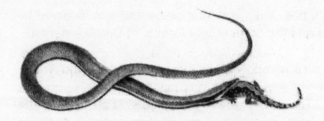

I INVITE YOU TO SMELL
WITH YOUR TONGUE

I was always taught that you smell with your nose, see with your eyes, hear with your ears, and you sense hot or cold with your skin.

But it happens that at times this may not be the case.

If we return to the world of the serpent, we discover that the poor thing does not have ears. In other words, it is deaf.

It has a nose but not to smell.

Instead it does have eyes with a dreadful and penetrating stare that it cannot hide because it doesn't have eye lids.

Then how does it hear the approaching of a human being?

Although you may not believe it, the serpent does not hear with its ears but with its jaws. It perceives heat not through its skin but through its nose and smells not with its nose but with its tongue.

Let's give attention to the latter. The tongue is forked and extraordinarily mobile. The serpent sticks out its tongue in order to be permeated with the smell of the animals which it is stalking. Thanks to the tongue, the serpent can detect and kill its prey.

I know you are not a serpent, although, people may say of someone that he has a viper's tongue. This is not your situation. However, I am inviting you to learn to smell with your tongue in the manner of a serpent.

When you say of someone: "To me that fellow stinks," although he may not smell, you are perhaps sensing a flaw in him with your skillful tongue and you make it known to others.

Paul, on the other hand, invites you and me to capture the good aroma of Christ which exudes from and envelops each person with an upright life, good deeds, and a radiant faith.

Perceive all of this goodness with your tongue and make it known to others, it is the work of God through His creatures.

THE FOUNTAINS OF LIFE

"**D**rink this herb tea and you will see that this will pass." This is what a grandmother says to the sick child, who does feel better after drinking the tea.

This scenario takes place everywhere, but especially among the indigenous people of Amazonia where it is quite common and significant.

For the natives, the jungle is a real pharmacy, a true fountain of health.

The jungle is not just a place of danger. It is rightly said that nature contains all of the poisons and all of the antidotes, as well as all of the illnesses and all of the remedies.

And because it contains all remedies, the destruction of the Amazon Jungle is tremendously damaging to all of humanity.

The Amazonian ecosystem contains a hidden potential for medicines that remedy the various ailments that burden humans.

This is why, by emulating the knowledge of the natives, a very special science called *Pharmacognosy* has emerged at universities.

This discipline is dedicated to the study of plants, insects, microorganisms, and of soils and trying to find healing substances in the laboratory that will be converted into fountains of life for humanity.

Appreciate this fountain of life.

Even more. Appreciate all of the fountains of life: from the vegetable and animal sources present in Amazonia, to the human and spiritual sources of the true love present in your heart, as well as, the fertile Word of the Lord and His Sacraments present in the Church.

And, remembering these fountains, join the psalmist and exclaim with him:

> The Lord is my Shepherd; I shall not want.
> He makes me to lie down in green pastures:
> He leads me besides the still waters.
> He restores my soul (Psalm 23, 1-3).

"The loss of forests and woodlands entails the loss of species which may constitute extremely important resources in the future, not only for food but also for curing disease and other uses." (LS 32)

CULTIVATE THE UNIVERSE

The town of Macondo, from Gabriel García Márquez's novel, *One Hundred Years of Solitude,* took measures to overcome the loss of memory.

Were all of the names of things being forgotten? Well, they even had to write the name of God on a wall to remember Him.

How terrible must it have been not to know the names of things, animals, people, or even the name of God!

This terrible sensation is being experienced today by tropical forest researchers. They know that there are thousands and thousands of unknown species of fauna and flora and that many are in danger of extinction even before they are named.

All tropical forests, primarily Amazonia, occupy only seven percent of the earth's surface but they possess half of the living species of the planet.

Fifty thousand species disappear from the forest each year without being studied, without having their benefits defined, and without even having been assigned a scientific name to identify them.

When God told Adam to give a name to the beings of creation, God was asking him to help create and cultivate the universe.

Each time that a scientist assigns a particular name to a species, he is also cooperating in this creation.

A scientist or not, you have been called upon to assist in the cultivation of the order of creation for the glory of God and the good of humanity. You are a part of humanity and much is expected from you.

YOU NEED AN AIRPLANE

"**M**any narrow passages of one or two kilometers in width, and nothing more. Where is the Amazon? Why can't I see anything else? You must lift yourself. A plane is needed. So I have not seen the Amazon. I will not speak any more about it."

The previous phrases are from a young man who was visiting the Amazon River. He wanted to capture more, much more, with each glance. But from the river itself, all he could see was just the two kilometer stretch that he had mentioned.

His conclusion is quite common. To see more you must elevate yourself. You need to be in an airplane.

This is due to a desire to see the totality, to capture everything from a wide-reaching perspective, and to admire the whole.

What the young man felt while viewing the Amazon River has been felt by many while facing the world in which we live.

They do not care to continue looking over a narrow horizon of merely two kilometers.

Curiously, they say the same thing as the young traveler in the Amazon: "You must elevate yourself." However, what they do isn't very common.

They don't take an airplane. They simply embrace a religious life.

When asked why they are retreating from the world, they respond: "We're not retreating from the world, we only want to see it in all its magnitude and we only distance ourselves in order to appreciate it better."

You must learn to look at yourself from a distance so that you can better see your qualities and faults along with your accomplishments and potential. Also, distance yourself from others, so that you may better appreciate who they are and what they do, and the quality of your relationships with them as well.

Finally, humble yourself before God so that you can recognize the reality of being a sinful human being. Then you can experience the abundant water of His mercy; it is as though you have submerged yourself into a "Divine Amazon."

A NEW CULTURE FOR A NEW JUNGLE

"A young woman traveling with us along the Amazon River sighed with satisfaction upon reaching the city of Manaus and passing a large and truly beautiful park.

Ah, finally we get to see nature!' she said. However, the young woman had just passed through the jungle."

This fragment from a traveler's account is quite significant.

Is it possible that after being deeply immersed in the thick of the jungle, she finally discovered nature when arriving at a city park? Yes, it is possible.

Nature cannot be separated from man nor man from nature.

But then, there is a relationship created between man and nature according to the specific type of nature which he experiences, and this becomes a part of the cultural being of each person.

Therefore, a park for someone who lives in the city can actually be nature, a pleasant space where people feel unbelievably relaxed.

But this same park is not nature for someone who lives and feels at home in the jungle. His relationship with the jungle is something different.

Presently one drama of the jungle is that it is being populated by those for whom true nature is a town's garden or park. For them, the jungle is a hostile environment which has to be eliminated.

I encourage you to deal with the jungle by improving your relationship with it. Don't let the city park be your only nature source but try to include the humid tropical forest that surrounds you. Don't look at the jungle as an enemy that must be destroyed. Let a new culture be born within you, a way of becoming different from the person who only sees nature in a city park or in a simple flower pot hanging from a balcony.

Incarnate yourself in the jungle in the same way that the Son of God was made flesh and became a man.

By almost disregarding His divine condition, He became one of us in this jungle of humanity which He loved and for whom He gave His life.

PROTECT YOUR INNER LIFE

They may be small, medium, or large. I am not talking about the size of ice-cream cones. I am talking about armadillos.

The smallest armadillo is called the rag tail. It has something resembling a straw tail, and as the saying goes, "He who has a straw tail should not get near a fire."

The medium armadillo does not have a special name, but it is the most common and is covered with patches on its head and tail. These are missing in the smaller armadillo, but they both have an interesting protective shell.

The third is called the giant. You might think that by being the largest and most powerful, it would not need as much protection.

However, that is not the case. As gigantic as it is, this armadillo also has to protect its vital interior organs. It neither shows off about being powerful nor exhibits airs of invulnerability when faced with danger. It recognizes its fragility and welcomes the protection of its shell.

You should imitate the armadillo by not exposing your inner life to the dangers of your surroundings. Create a protective shell for yourself, not to isolate yourself from others, but to protect the most important part of your inner life: With the presence of God in your heart, this divine life that makes you a son or daughter of God, brother or sister to Christ, and a true Christian.

This is a treasure worthy of protection, not by just any shield, but by one made of firm convictions, solid values, and unwavering attitudes.

I don't mean to minimize you, but you, too, have a straw tail. Do not play with the fire of temptation but distance yourself from it. For he who loves danger perishes from danger.

Cherish your inner life and, by emulating the armadillo, defend it with a shield made of values, convictions, and attitudes which will protect it well.

NOT JUST A SIMPLE CHILDREN'S STORY

It may seem to be a simple story. It was written in honor of Chico Méndez, an environmentalist and defender of Amazonia. But it is more than a story. It is the expression of the drama of the living world of Amazonia. The author, Lynne Cherry, entitled it *The Great Kapok Tree* (*La grandiosa Ceiba*).

"The man took the ax he carried and struck the trunk of the tree. Whack!

…Soon the man grew tired. He sat down to rest at the foot of the great Kapok tree. Before he knew it, the heat and hum of the forest lulled him to sleep.

A boa constrictor lived in the Kapok tree. He slithered down its trunk to where the man was sleeping. Then the huge snake slid very close to the man and hissed in his ear: 'Senhor, this tree is a tree of miracles. It is my home where generations of my ancestors have lived. Do not chop it down.'

A bee buzzed in the sleeping man's ear: 'Senhor, my hive is in the Kapok tree. I fly from tree to tree and flower to flower collecting pollen. In this way I pollinate the trees and flowers throughout this rain forest. You see, all living things depend on one another.'

A troupe of monkeys scampered down from the canopy of the Kapok tree. They chattered to the sleeping man: 'Senhor, we have seen the ways of man. You chop down one tree then come back for another and another. The roots of all of these great trees wither and die, and there will be nothing left to hold the earth in place. When the heavy rains come, the soil will be washed away and the forest will become a desert.'

A toucan, a macaw, and a cock-of-the-rock flew down from the canopy. 'Senhor!' squawked the toucan, 'you must not cut down this tree. We have flown over the rain forest and have seen what happens once you begin to chop down the trees. Many people settle on the land. They set fires to clear the underbrush, and soon the forest disappears. Where once there was life and beauty only black and smoldering ruins remain.'

A bright and small tree frog crawled along the edge of a leaf. In a squeaky voice he piped in the man's ear: 'Senhor, a ruined rain forest means ruined lives…many ruined lives. You will leave many of us homeless if you chop down this great Kapok tree.'

Many other animals took turns to come down to whisper in the sleeping man's ear from the jaguar whose food always came from that tree to the porcupines in need of oxygen from the tropical forest; from anteaters worried about their future without their tree to a three-toed sloth who spoke in her deep and lazy voice: 'Senhor, how much is beauty worth? If you destroy the beauty of the rain forest, on what would you feast your eyes?'

A child from the Yanomamo tribe who lived in the rain forest knelt over the sleeping man. He murmured in his ear: 'Senhor, when you awake, please look upon us all with new eyes.'

The man awoke and before him stood the rain forest child, and all around him, staring, were the creatures who depended upon the great Kapok tree. What wondrous and rare animals they were!

The man stood and picked up his ax. He swung back his arm as though to strike the tree. Suddenly he stopped. He turned and looked at the animals and the child. He hesitated for a moment. Then he dropped the ax and walked out of the rain forest." (*The Great Kapok Tree, a Tale from the Amazon Rain Forest*)

It is only a dream. But remember that God has communicated great messages through dreams. Such as when He told Joseph: "Pick up the Baby and take Him to Egypt because Herod wants to kill Him."

And this message is also for you, a message of life in favor of those who are about to perish and for whom you can do something right now by emulating Joseph who without waiting, not even for a second, took the Baby and his mother and began their journey.

Fables help to make children fall asleep. This fable, instead, helps to make adults awaken and act immediately in favor of life in the Amazon jungle.

"There has been a tragic rise in the number of migrants seeking to flee from the growing poverty caused by environmental degradation. They are not recognized by international conventions as refugees; they bear the loss of the lives they have left behind, without enjoying any legal protection whatsoever. Sadly, there is widespread indifference to such suffering, which is even now taking place throughout our world." (LS 25)

EXTRAVAGANT

I f the disproportioned beaks of toucans were solid, their owners would not be able to carry them.

Granted, the beaks are not solid. Nevertheless, we cannot help thinking that they are rather excessive.

And, if we add their strident screeching to their overgenerous beaks we arrive to the conclusion that Amazonian toucans are really extravagant.

The relationship between the size of the beak and its full function is not entirely understood. Toucans may understand, but for us it seems like a showy hindrance.

My conclusion is, and I repeat myself, that toucans are really extravagant.

Maybe they have good reason to disagree. So, to keep from exaggeration, perhaps we should limit ourselves to considering them as symbols of extravagant people. No doubt, there are a few.

It is believed that an extravagant person does not have a healthy relationship between what he is and what he wants to be. You can say that this person flies too high or as the Italians say: "He wants to take a step much longer than his legs permit."

What is the reason behind people's extravagance? Possibly, it is a desire to be noticed, not for their screeching like toucans, but for their grand, even if unrealistic, goals.

In a less complex situation it can be just a case of immaturity. In a more complex case, such as schizophrenia, it is perhaps an attempt to overcome an inferiority complex which accompanies extravagant persons and inflicts suffering upon them.

When you become aware of the love that God has for you and the mission He has entrusted unto you, your extravagance should diminish. You will not need it since you have discovered the worth that you have in God's eyes and in the eyes of those who love you.

A RIVER
WITHOUT
A COURSE

O bviously it has a course. You cannot conceive
of a river without a course. But the truth is
that the Amazon River has course problems
because of the tremendous floods that often occur.

In Amazonia there are two distinct periods of the year: the
dry season and the rainy season. The first produces a great
drop in the water level and the second a great rise.

The torrential rain generates an overflowing of water which
triggers minor floods that cover strips of land a few yards
wide or great floods that can cover 6 to 9 miles on either
side of the river, depending upon the height of the interior
lands. These floods usually cause serious problems for
agriculture, cattle, wild fauna, and pasture land.

You can say that the floods do serve to fertilize the soil, which is true, but at the same time some living creatures face serious dangers or at least many troubles and discomforts. For them it would be better if the Amazon River did not overflow so much.

This is a simple wish, but the reality is different. The same thing happens with love. How wonderful it would be if love were always like a river which maintains its course. But at times, love may lose its course and then problems begin. If the force of the river can help us to understand the force of love, then the flooding or overflowing helps us to understand that the boundary of love is respect.

True love must always be accompanied by respect. When the limits of respect are transgressed, love can produce pain and generate suffering instead of happiness. Just as a river needs a true course, true love needs respect.

Love is like the Amazon River during the flood season with its heavy flow and strong current. When love becomes a blind force, it is necessary to establish order and to regulate the course. Respect is the course and order of love. Only respect wins the love and trust of another person.

Just as rivers have high times and low times, times of abundance and times of shortage, people in love have their own special rhythms, their winter and summer, and their ups and downs. Those rhythms must be respected as a part of truly loving someone. After all, do we really expect a mango tree to steadily produce mangoes the entire year?

TRUST WHAT COMES FROM ABOVE

Bromeliads and ferns do not grow roots in the ground. They belong to the family of the epiphytes which live on the trunks and branches of other species.

I suppose that their lives are not easy since they are not able to extract nutrients from the humus of the soil, no matter how rich or poor it may be.

But, as commonly said, when one door closes another opens. Thus, bromeliads which cannot rely on what they get from below must place their trust on what they get from above.

This is why the leaves of bromeliads and ferns have a special formation to facilitate the accumulation of water and organic material which falls from above.

The leaves are organized around a central axis shaped like an inverted umbrella. They also have orifices which regulate the absorption of water according to the needs of each plant.

Bromeliads: What better image can we find to illustrate the needs of the human spirit?

Without trusting excessively on what comes from below, the human spirit knows how to be receptive to that which comes from above, the refreshing Living Water of God's revelations, the richness of His Word, and the Grace of his Sacraments.

It was said by a Saint:

In dealing with material things, I want to be a channel so that everything passes through me without my being attached to it. In dealing with spiritual things, I want to be like a shell which receives and preserves them in its heart.

Of Mary it is said: "She kept all things in her heart." (Lukas 2, 51)

What a marvelous bromeliad: The Mother of the Lord!

ADDITIONAL
SUPPORT

This is what happens to them for exaggerating. But no. It is better to say that this occurs to them for aspirating to reach so high.

I am not referring to merchants, nor to bankers, politicians, or beauty queens.

I am referring exclusively to the trees of Amazonia. Their trunks grow excessively tall because of their desire and their need to reach the light.

However, their roots do not guarantee stability since they have to spread just under the surface of the soil in order to feed on the thin layer of humus.

Thus, the tree has to find additional support, something that serves as a vertical counterforce in order to prop it up.

This structure of support can also be built horizontally in the manner of a thick root called bamba or buttress. In this way, the immense tree surmounts the limitations of the fragility of the soil and the overwhelming force of the occasional but destructive stormy winds of Amazonia.

This is the option that it must take if it wants to become a great tree, and it is very much like to the option that a person must take to grow to become a great human being.

With realism and humility, a person who wants to excel in the personal, and communal or societal field should know how to seek additional supporting structures. Structures of support along with individual resolve and effort help a person achieve the greatest heights of maturity. Especially in the spiritual life, where cultural guides are not exactly the best support, it is important, even indispensable, to allow yourself to be supported and guided in the advancement toward the heights of the spirit.

Christ offered himself as a formidable support for the human spirit and something more than a support:

Live on in me, as I do in you. No more can a branch bear fruit in itself apart from the vine, than you can bear fruit apart from me. I am the vine; you are the branches. He who lives in me and I in him, will produce abundantly. (John 15, 4-5)

Do you want more support? Jesus himself will offer it to you: "You will receive power when the Holy Spirit comes down upon you; then you are to be my witnesses." (Acts 1, 8)

THE POWER OF KNOTS

Do you need a ladder; it's always present.

Do you need a scaffold; it can't be beaten.

Do you need a pretty guard-rail for the house; everyone thinks of it.

Do you need to put up a flag or an antenna; there is no better alternative.

Do we need to build a house; it is the first thing that comes to mind.

How very useful *guadua* bamboo is.

It is true that the natives seldom use it since they prefer to use palm tree wood. But, they do craft ritual objects such as ceremonial items, staffs, trumpets, and so forth from the *guadua*.

Guadua is a gigantic Gramineae plant of the bamboo family. That is why the scientific name, *Tribe bambuseae*, is unique.

It is massive in height even though it is quite thin. When you look at it you wonder why it does not break. What is its secret?

There is no secret. It is well known that its strength lies in the knots that interrupt its ascending column every twenty inches or so.

If it were totally smooth, it would break more easily. But its length is crossed horizontally every so often by knots in the fashion of solid rings. This is a property of the *guadua* and the bamboo family throughout the world.

Precisely, it was bamboo trees which inspired a Japanese person to reveal his feelings about prayer. He said:

«Everyday activities are like a bamboo cane. The knots give strength to the cane. These knots are those moments of explicit prayer which interrupt the daily activity and for a moment cut off the flow of our life. Prayers are like the material of the *guadua* knot: They help cope with the worries and anxieties that are interwoven into our life each day.»

The days of our lives are similar to the spaces between one knot and the next in a *guadua* cane. Prayer in our lives is like the power of the knot in the *guadua*, a power that is effective because it divides the cane horizontally.

Do not merely say that the whole of your life is a prayer, thus concluding that you never need to pray. Decide to let the flow of your life be parted by those powerful knots, by those special moments, small or large, which suspend your existence and place you with your open hands before God.

TREE OF LIFE

Test: A word taken from English which is now a part of the Spanish language meaning exam.

Nowadays, they test you for everything. They want to know if you are slow or intelligent, if you are composed or restless, if you are normal or neurotic, if you are clever in an activity or if you are all thumbs in that field.

In Amazonia there are ways to test if you are an offspring of the culture or a stranger to it.

If you are faced with Amazonian culture and you feel familiar with it and at ease with what it offers, the result is positive. You are considered as a true son or daughter of this culture.

If you feel uncomfortable or even have a desire to reject, minimize, or ridicule it, you are far from being considered a true son or daughter of Amazonian culture.

But, what is the tree of life? In the difficult language of the scientist it is called *Mauritia flexuosa*. In everyday language it is called *canangucha*. It is a palm tree, one of two thousand species of palms that are found in the tropical world.

For indigenous communities this palm has become so important that they call it "The tree of life." And they are right.

The *canangucha* has innumerable uses which can be applied to a variety of activities. The orange pulp of the fruit is very nutritious with a high content of fats, proteins, and carbohydrates. It is consumed directly or can be processed into different forms in order to produce a cooking oil or even a fermented beverage called *chicha*.

Fiber of excellent quality can be extracted from the young leaves from which cords, hammocks, and baskets are made. The trunk also serves as material for building homes.

Well-deserved is its name, "Tree of life."

Here we also find another tree which has the opposite name, "The tree of death." It is the coca tree from which cocaine is extracted. The misuse of this tree is made by those who have not become true children of the Amazon culture.

When faith is made an intrinsic part of culture, *canangucha* will be more highly ranked as a symbol of life and will be reminiscent of the heart of our Creator and Provider, The God of Life.

VAINGLORY

The canoe slides quickly down the river. It is an everyday trip in Amazonia where the most common vehicle is the canoe.

In the course of the trip, a wake trails the canoe. This track in the river is caused by the displacement of the water with the passing of the canoe.

The trace is fleeting. It lingers for just a few seconds and then the water returns to its calm state. Not a hint of a wake will reappear.

No canoe would boast about such a weak sign of its presence.

But perhaps, human beings might glorify themselves with such a simple, fleeting, and worthless wake.

A slug like the one which just entered my office while leaving behind a trace of slime of little value can teach us about vainglory.

Staring at it, I cannot help but remember the literary image by an Italian poet who expressed his thoughts in Roman verse:

> The silly slug of vainglory
> Who slid across a monument
> Saw his slime and said: "This is no fantasy,
> Today, I leave my mark on history."

The fleeting wake in the river and the shiny thread that the slug leaves behind may at times reflect the useless vainglory of your inflated ego.

Do not let yourself be deceived by those frail signs of feeble vainglory. If you truly aspire to glory, not to vainglory, follow the example of the humble Apostle Paul. He knew how to glorify himself for what he did, not because it was the work of his hands, but because it was exclusively the work of the Lord.

Paul used good judgment when he said: "He who wants to glorify himself, glorify in the Lord."

THE MADHOUSE

O nly a few times in history has a dream appeared with such a facade of reality. Fantasy was turned loose and everyone swallowed the story.

I am referring to the first Europeans who set foot in Amazonia. Perhaps they were accustomed to accepting as truth what others had simply dreamed. The dreamers were authors such as Pliny, Herodotus, Arabian fiction writers, and authors of books of chivalry.

Lake Guatavita, near Bogotá where the *Cacique* or Indian chief submerged himself with his body covered in gold dust, set in motion the myth of El Dorado.

Soon, the longed for El Dorado became identified as a fabulous lake in Amazonia called Parimé. It was believed to be larger than the Caspian Sea, and cartographers painted it on maps for many centuries, thus assuring others that it was a marvelous reality.

El Dorado, the person who covered himself in gold, now resided near Parimé in the city of Manoa, the most beautiful of those cities conquered by the Spaniards. The Amazonian El Dorado, Lake Parimé, and the fabulous city of Manoa, were all fabrications which were fully accepted out of simple naivety.

Were these the only tales? No! Also in Amazonia were the supposedly headless men with their mouths in the middle of their chest, giants taller than ten feet and dwarfs "no larger than tender babies."

As if these were not enough, even a century later there was talk about people who had their feet on backwards, so that when they wanted to draw near, the only thing that they could manage was to step away.

How many heads fell, one after another, with the dreams engendered by Amazonia! There were the heads of heroes and heads of bandits: Gonzalo de Pizarro, Lope de Aguirre, and Walter Raleigh just to mention a few.

In addition to greed, they were also moved by an unchangeable yearning for fantasy.

With the sound works of La Condamine, Humboldt, Bondpland and others, Amazonia would finally be free from the domain of these dreams. These illusions would no longer have such authority and acceptance in Amazonia.

And, although imagination may always be needed, let us hope it will not be the last word in the mysterious jungles of your life.

Let your life be enlightened by reason and faith.

VERTICAL
AND
HORIZONTAL

D o you think that I am trying to solve a word puzzle? That's not the case. The fact is that I want to talk to you about rain.

Showers in Amazonia are abundant and continuous. They often come accompanied by deafening thunder and frightening flashes of lightning.

In a downpour in Amazonia you had better find yourself under a roof; otherwise you will be drenched to your bones.

But the complication with the Amazon rain is that it does not usually fall vertically as in most places on earth. Many times, rain falls horizontally, and although you may have a very good roof, rain knows how to get in through windows or any other opening that gives it the chance.

That is why roofs are usually made with large eaves which cover an extension almost equivalent to the size of the house itself. This helps to protect us from the horizontal rain.

There are other types of showers from which we don't need to defend ourselves, although at times we may fear them.

These are the rains from God.

The water of His gifts falls on us like rain, sometimes vertically and at other times horizontally.

Vertically, when His grace falls on us through His Word, the Sacraments, prayer, and whenever we open ourselves to God's influence.

Horizontally, when His grace falls on us by way of everyday events through the love of our dear ones, or in the acts of service by which we draw ourselves near to the needy.

Don't use a roof, large eaves, or an umbrella to keep out God's rain. Let His water drench you to the very marrow of your bones.

THE ONE WITH THE SEVEN MOUTHS

I t's not a monster, at least, not entirely. It's a cow.

But it's neither the laughing nor the crying cow. Nor is it the milk cow in a popular song which claims not to be an ordinary cow. This is a cow with seven mouths.

No more or no less. And it wouldn't matter if it had seven or seventy mouths if each mouth didn't have to consume a lot of grass.

And where do you find a cow with such a deformity? This is easy to answer: in Amazonia.

And in which pasture in Amazonia can we see such a strange bovine? This is also easy to answer: in all.

All of the cows in Amazonia have seven mouths and they consume a portion of the grass with each mouth. Now, here is the problem. Although being only one cow, each eats for seven.

Perhaps I should quickly explain myself.

The Amazonian cow consumes grass through its mouth; but it also damages the pasture by stepping heavily with its four hooves, each hoof crushes the grass deplorably. And, as if this is not enough, where the manure falls, the grass becomes rotten. You can say the same thing about the urine. This makes a total of seven consumers of grass.

Count and you will discover that although there is only one cow that eats through one mouth, it has six other consumers of grass. This is why a cow requires a lot of space.

Where are we going to find all of the pasture land that each cow needs? From the jungle itself! Trees are cut down, fauna dwindles, rivers are altered, and the soil is damaged. But all of this doesn't seem to matter, provided that her majesty the cow, being such an avid consumer of grass, has enough open space for her seven mouths.

But you are probably saying that I'm being unfair to the poor silent cow which, after all, has no other choice. This is true. So let's absolve the cow and instead let's call into judgment its owner and master.

All of the consumption of this innocent cow is simply a reflection of another consumer, the professional cattlemen in search of land, boundless land, because making boundless profits is their primary rule.

Be careful; don't let this cow become a symbol of your life by being fully dedicated to consumerism.

"We can note the rise of a false or superficial ecology which bolsters complacency and a cheerful recklessness. As often occurs in periods of deep crisis which require bold decisions, we are tempted to think that what is happening is not entirely clear. Superficially, apart from a few obvious signs of pollution and deterioration, things do not look that serious, and the planet could continue as it is for some time. Such evasiveness serves as a license to carrying on with our present lifestyles and models of production and consumption. This is the way human beings contrive to feed their self-destructive vices: trying not to see them, trying not to acknowledge them, delaying the important decisions and pretending that nothing will happen." (LS 59)

DOMESTIC
ANIMAL
OR WILD
ANIMAL

Everyone would like to keep one at home with the hope that it would behave like a well-trained little kitty. I am speaking of the ocelot from the humid tropical jungles.

The ocelot's color is so beautiful that people want it to adorn their patio at home, not in the terrible form of a skin hanging on a wall, but in the beauty of a living creature.

Not just the ocelot, we could say the same thing about the Amazonian coati, the fox, and many other mammals of the jungle.

The fact is that these are wild animals and as such, they prefer the open life of the jungle to the confinement of a house where they will die in a short period of time.

This doesn't happen with a cat or a dog. Both of them being domestic animals live happily indoors. Furthermore, they love being in the kitchen next to a generous cook.

Wild animals usually flee from a house, while domestic animals, as the name implies, enjoy being in the house.

There is nothing strange about this situation. You may even say that this is such a plain and obvious truth that it is almost not worth writing about.

But look to a higher level, look at yourself.

Look to the House of the Father and ask yourself: Do I consider that I am more like a wild animal who flees from His House or like a domesticated one who feels at ease within His House?

You will probably reply that at times you feel like the former and at times like the latter. This is not unusual.

Either way, you should look to the Psalms once in a while. There you will find the testimony of people who sing about the joy of dwelling in the House of the Lord. Here is an example:

> «I have asked the Lord for one thing
> One thing only do I want
> To live in the house of the Lord
> All the days of my life». (Psalm 27)

ALL PRAISE BE YOURS, MY LORD!

May the birds of the jungle sing the glory of God, and the humid forests announce His Greatness!

The life of the forests and the song of the birds are a sublime hymn to the Creator of the universe.

Not just the birds and the forests. But also human beings, in admiration of the immense richness of the biological order, burst forth into a song of enthusiastic praise.

What better conclusion for this work, than to invite the man who, like no one else, loved Creation and from this love he forged a glorious staircase to God. I am referring to St. Francis of Assisi. I invite you to delight yourself in his "Chant of the Creatures."

All praise be yours, my Lord,
through all your creatures,
And first through my Brother Sun,
Who brings the day; and light you give to us
through him.
How beautiful is he, how radiant in his splendor!
Of you, Most High, he bears the likeness.

All praise be yours, my Lord, through Sister Water,
So useful, humble, precious, and pure.

All praise be yours, my Lord, through Sister Earth,
our mother,
Who feeds us in her sovereignty and produces
Various fruits with colored flowers and herbs.

All creatures praise and bless my Lord,
Serve him with tenderness and a humble heart,
Thank him for his gifts, sing of his creation. Amen.

"'LAUDATO SI, mi Signore'- 'Praise be to you, my Lord.' In the words of this beautiful canticle, Saint Francis of Assisi reminds us that our common home is like a sister with whom we share our life and a beautiful mother who opens her arms to embrace us." (LS 1)

ANIMALS OF THE AMAZON JUNGLE WHO KINDLY AGREED TO BE A PART OF THIS WORK

1. **Antbirds** *Formicariidae* (Formicarido)
2. **Biting miges** *Culicoides* (Jején)
3. **Black Curassow** *Crax alector* (Paujil)
4. **Black-capped Capuchin** *Cebus apella* (Maicero Cachudo)
5. **Blue morpho butterfly** *Morpho* (Mariposa Azul)
6. **Bullet ant** *Paraponera* (Conga)
7. **Bushmaster venomous snake** *Lachesis muta* (Verrugosa)
8. **Capybara** *Hydrochaerus hydrocaeris* (Chigüiro)
9. **Chigoe flea or chigger** *Tunga penetrans* (Nigua)
10. **Coral snake** *Micrurus* (Coral)
11. **Cougar or Mountain Lion** *Felis Concolor* (Puma)
12. **Dwarf Monkey** *Cebuella pygmaea* (Tití pielroja)
13. **Giant Anteater or Ant Bear** *Myrmecophaga tridactyla* (Oso hormiguero)
14. **Great White Egret** *Casmodorodius albus* (Garza blanca)
15. **Harpy Eagle** *Harpia harpyia* (Águila Miquera)
16. **Hummingbird** *Glaucis* (Colibrí)
17. **Jaguar** *Panthera Onca* (Tigre mariposa)
18. **Leaf-cutter ant** *Atta* (Arriera)
19. **Little spotted cat or Oncilla** *Felis Trigrina* (Tigrillo)
20. **Lowland Paca** *Cuniculus paca* (Lapa)
21. **Muscovy Duck** *Carina moschata* (Pato real)
22. **Nine-banded armadillo** *Dasypus novemcinctus* (Armadillo)
23. **Otter** *Lutra enudris* (Nutria)
24. **Palm weevil** *Rhina palmorum* (Mojojoi)
25. **Pirahna** *Serrasalmus* (Piraña)
26. **Poison-dart frog** *Dendrobates* (Rana venenosa)
27. **Red-rumped Cacique** *Cacicus* (Arrendajo)

28. **Six-tubercled river turtle** *Podocnemis sextuberculata* (Tortuga cupiso)
29. **South American coati** *Nasua nasua* (Cusumbo)
30. **South American Tapir** *Tapirus terrestris* (Danta)
31. **Three-toed sloth** *Bradypus* (Perico Ligero)
32. **Toucan** *Ramphastus* (Tucán)
33. **Vampiro bat** *Desmodus rotundus* (Vampiro)
34. **Vine snake** *Oxybelix* (Bejuca)